Preface v

Acknowledgements xi

Chapter 1 - The Early Years...1

Chapter 2 - The Hanya Holm Years 17

Chapter 3 - A Bird Must Fly Away...31

Chapter 4 - Touch and Go, the Musical..48

Chapter 5 - Think of Your Buttocks as Apples and Prick them with Toothpicks - The Birth of Mary Anthony's School and Company 63

Chapter 6 - Hard Work through Trial and Error Pays Off........94

Chapter 7 - The Golden Years..103

Chapter 8 - Mary's Philosophy..137

Chapter 9 - Greedy Landlord and Forging Ahead...................145

Chapter 10 - Mary's Cats 151

Chapter 11 - Fire Island 155

Chapter 12 - Letters to Mary..161

Preface

Years ago, I saw a Modern Dance Tree, and I was quite disturbed that it didn't have Mary Anthony's name on it. The tree featured Mary Wigman, below her was Hanya Holm, and below Hanya was Alwin Nikolais. Yet, Mary had taught Alwin Nikolais when she was teaching a full curriculum at the Hanya Holm School in the early 1940s. Mary's name should have been under Hanya Holm, followed by Alwin Nikolais. In the very early 80s, I was teaching at the Jefferson High School of the Performing Arts in Portland, Oregon. Alwin Nikolais was a guest artist for a week or two. I sat with him during several lunches, and we discussed this very topic. He agreed that her name should have been on that tree and that she should be recognized.

Dancing for the Mary Anthony Dance Theatre in the early 1970s was a dream. Her classes and choreography felt wonderful on my body. My training before dancing with Mary was ballet and the Martha Graham dance technique. Mary's lyrical and theatrical technique felt like a combination of these two realms; at the same time, her instruction added a new dimension. The way that Mary composes her classes is amazing. You don't just do steps. Her inspiration comes from art museums, performances, literature, philosophers; indeed, just the beauty of each day. She brings this inspiration to every class with themes that speak of the soul. I was so fortunate to have trained with her and danced as a soloist in her company.

I have heard several important dance people describe Mary Anthony as a great pedagogue, but not a choreographer. It is difficult to pass judgment on the quality of the choreography in which you are dancing—as any dancer can tell you, you are an instrument for the choreographer. A dancer, hopefully, doesn't pass judgment on the choreographer's work. So perhaps I am prejudiced when I say that I think Mary is a fabulous choreographer. But, I don't think I am prejudiced. Many years after I had danced for Mary, Hunter College hosted a 40th anniversary concert for her company. I attended as an observer, like others in the audience. What I saw was breathtaking and beautiful. Witnessing the 40th anniversary performance as a member of the audience validated for me that she is a great choreographer.

Thus, I wanted to write Mary's book. And, I wanted to write a biography that was reader friendly and full of rich information about a person who has touched so many lives. I have never written anything other than my MFA theses at the University of Oklahoma and a scattering of papers and articles, but I decided to take on this project. I actually asked her if I could do so when I was pregnant with my second child. That was in 1981. Mary agreed, and her suggestion was to connect with Tom Wetmore, one of her cherished students, as he had recorded seven interviews with her. He was writing a paper on her for an assignment as part of obtaining his Master's in Dance from New York University.

My next step was to transcribe the tapes. Originally, they were on the old-fashioned reel-to-reel tapes. Fortunately, the cassette tape had debuted, and I made copies of the reel-to-reel onto cassettes. The process of transcribing took me a long time—several years, as a matter of fact. I was raising two children, and I was teaching full time. In addition to the tapes, I undertook some of my own research at the Lincoln Center Performing Arts Library, where actually I couldn't find much.

Making several trips to New York to spend time with Mary was imperative. I took at least one to two trips each year. Working with Mary is like keeping up with a busy bumblebee; she's always on the run. She loaned me programs, reviews, and photos, which I have scanned. It has taken all of these things to describe her life. And she herself gave the book its title: *A Dancer's Journey: It All Began with a Lie*. In her childhood, Mary experienced people who told and lived lies, and she wanted no part of that. Her ultimate reaction to those lies became the basis for her journey toward the truth of dance and art.

At this writing, Mary is 95 years old. An inspiration, she is still teaching and taking class, which is absolutely amazing. She has survived many financial hardships and other challenges. Many people in her shoes would have been so discouraged that they would have taken a university position if only for the financial security and benefits. She has been offered several university positions, but has always wanted to stay and continue working in New York City.

Mary became the dancer she did all because of the scholarship that Hanya Holm gave her. The tradition continued when Mary opened her own studio. Over many years, students have been awarded Mary Anthony scholarships, where they received her fabulous training in exchange for helping at the desk and cleaning, but also for their talent. Many of these scholarship dancers have gone on to have professional careers in dance. Clearly, Mary Anthony has touched 100s of lives. At Mary's 95th birthday celebration on November 11, 2011, the guests included all the generations of friends, dancers, and students she has touched. An honor was bestowed on her by the President of the Borough of Manhattan, Scott M Stringer, naming November 11, 2011, **Mary Anthony Celebration Day**. The declaration said,

We are proud to acknowledge those individuals who have devoted their time and talents to enriching New York City's cultural community, and whose artistic influence and example are an inspiration to our city; and

Whereas: Mary Anthony is an extraordinary presence in the dance community and the artistry and depth of her choreography is timeless; and

Whereas: A second generation modern dancer, Mary Anthony has cultivated numerous professional dancers, artistic directors, and choreographers as well as developed and inspired hundreds of individuals since her studio's inception in 1954; and

Whereas: Mary Anthony, an internationally renowned dancer continues to share her artistic talents with her community at the Mary Anthony Dance Studio at 736 Broadway in Manhattan;

Now therefore, I Scott M. Stringer do hereby congratulate and commend Mary Anthony on the occasion of her 95th birthday and proclaim this Friday, November 11, 2011 **Mary Anthony Celebration Day** in the Borough of Manhattan.

It is with great honor that I share the journey of Mary Anthony.

Mary Anthony, photo by © Michel Delsol

Mary Anthony, photo by © Michel Delsol

Mary Anthony at her 95th Brithday, November 11, 2011

Mary Anthony with her Proclamation, November 11, 2011

Mary Anthony's 95th Birthday party, November 11, 2011

Acknowledgements

With complete humility, I wish to acknowledge many people who have assisted and helped with this book chronicling the life of Mary Anthony.

During the time I was an associate professor in Dance at Oklahoma City University, I worked with honor student Ashley Rivers, who was interested in writing and in my book. She was a performance major and is a beautiful dancer. During her time at Oklahoma City University, Ashley assisted me by organizing all the reviews and programs in chronological order, as well as organizing the many photographs that depicted Mary's full and rich life. Presently, Ashley Rivers is a Calderwood Fellow in writing at Emerson College, where she is nonfiction editor of *Redivider Journal*. A regular contributor to *Dance Spirit* magazine, she also writes for *Dance, Pointe* and *Dance Teacher*. This past year, Ashley has combed through the chapters with me, clarifying, correcting, and assisting in the research of historical material. Ashley, I can never thank you enough for all the hours you devoted to assisting me.

Thank you to Tom Wetmore who completed the seven long interviews with Mary on reel-to-reel tape in 1980. Those tapes were invaluable in capturing so much of Mary's life. One could hear Mary's highs and Mary's lows on the recordings. Originally, Tom did the interviews for a paper he was writing for part of his Master's Degree in Dance at New York University. Little did he know how important those tapes would become.

When I began transcribing Tom's tapes, it was a slow, tedious process. I would listen and then write in long hand what I heard. Later, I typed up my notes on a typewriter. This generation of the computer age would have been wonderful in the 80s and early 90s. Michelle Sterling helped me type the notes from my long hand, and I am eternally grateful.

Virginia ("Ginny") Nill Jinks has been a tremendous help with the book. She looks after Mary with such adoration and love. Mary has always loved the ocean, and Ginny takes her on little excursions so Mary can touch the sand, hear the waves, and smell the ocean in the breeze. As we have been working on Mary's book, Ginny has read the drafts of the chapters to Mary for accuracy. Ginny even rented a car and drove Mary to Philadelphia, taking total care of her, so that Mary could be at the Philly Fringe Festival to view rehearsals and see her work *Threnody* performed on

Gwendolyn Bye's dance company, Dancefusion. Gwendolyn danced in Mary's company for 14 years and is restaging Mary's outstanding choreography to keep it alive.

Another dancer who is helping keep Mary's choreography alive is Pasqualina Noel from France. She is a former dancer of the Martha Graham Ensemble and the Pearl Lang Dance Company. In January 2010, Mary watched Pasqualina rehearsing with Ethel Winter, and subsequently chose her to dance the solo *Lady Macbeth*. Pasqualina performed it several times in France. The French Ministry of Culture gave her a grant to notate the solo in Benesh Notation. When the notation is finished, it will be housed in the Centre National de la Danse in Paris, and another copy will be housed in the Dance Notation Bureau.

Victoria Geduld also conducted some interviews with Mary about her life for a paper that she was writing for research on the New Dance Group, with which Mary had been involved. Her interviews added extra information to Tom Wetmore's interviews.

Daniel Maloney has been wonderful to Mary. He lives in a loft space directly below Mary, and he is always looking in on her to make sure she is well. Besides being a dancer and choreographer, he is also a physical therapist. Part of Mary's prescription from her doctor is physical therapy. Because Daniel is right there in her building, she rides the elevator down to receive her needed physical therapy two or three times each week. Many times her Medicare doesn't pay for this, but he still gives Mary the much-needed therapy.

Another thank you goes to Cynthia Noe. Not only has she been encouraging me these many years, but she escorted me numerous times to Mary's studio to comb through and organize the multitudes of photographs that I later scanned.

When I taught at the University of Illinois in Champaign/Urbana, Patricia Knowles was the dance chair. Following my suggestion, she brought Mary Anthony in as a guest artist. The department loved her work so much that they continued to host her for many years. I have the greatest gratitude to Ms. Knowles for not only helping share Mary's art, but also for continuing to stay in touch with Mary and financially support her work.

Lastly, I want to thank Joseph Gifford for his insightful interview with me; Donald McKayle for his exciting interview; the Paul Sanasardo interview (1984) of his admiration of Mary; Ráchel Lowery for designing the cover of the book (artwork by Alfred Van Leon); and to my husband Richard Weil, who has been encouraging through this entire journey. Thank you to all the people I have not named above. It took everyone.

A Dancer's Journey "It All Started With A Lie"   *xiii*

Ashley Rivers

Mary Anthony center front, left to right Virginia Nill Jinks, Mary Price Boday, and Gwendolyn Bye 2011

CHAPTER 1

The Early Years

Why would a young woman leave her hometown and move to a place where she has no friends or family? Growing up in Newport, Kentucky, Mary Anthony had been inspired during trips across the river to Cincinnati, Ohio where she was audience to operas, symphonies, and plays. Once, she saw Martha Graham perform a solo concert with Louis Horst playing the piano. From these artistic excursions, Mary knew there was a bigger place for the arts than where she grew up. She was also conflicted and frustrated with the lies that she witnessed at home. So, as a sophomore in college, Mary Anthony fled her Kentucky home for New York City with just a single suitcase.

Mary Anthony was born on November 11, 1916 and was an only child. Newport, Kentucky is located at the confluence of the Ohio and Licking Rivers. A borderline "Southern" town, it is laid out in the shape of an Irish cross, with the northern edge reaching the Ohio River, which flooded often. A friend of Mary's lived in that northern part of town, and after every flood, the Red Cross gave them new furniture and new wallpaper for their homes. Living on the eastern part of town, Mary felt fortunate to spend her young years in the middle-class section that buttressed an exclusive neighborhood adorned by large, shady trees. Mary described it this way: "If you have ever read James Agree's *A Death in the Family*, there is a prologue which takes place in Knoxville, Tennessee, and you can just apply that to [the eastern] part of my home town of Newport, Kentucky." Agree's novel takes place in a southern town with quiet neighborhood evenings and centers around a man looking back to his childhood. The novel focuses on marital love and loss, religion, and America in 1915—just one year before Mary was born.[1]

During her childhood, Mary was never allowed to go to the other side of the railroad tracks, which was the western part, as it was people with laborers, African Americans, and the poor. Many worked for the steel company and were sometimes called "River Rats." In the southern part of this area was the steel mill for the town of Newport.

Both interested in music, Mary's parents met at a music club. Her mother played the zither, a musical instrument with strings across a sound board that one plucked with the fingers. Mary's father played the mandolin. According to Mary, had they met in the 21st century, her parents never would have gotten married. They were very different individuals. "My mother was an exceptionally creative lady who married the wrong man in the wrong time," said Mary. Her mother was vibrant and artistic. She would design patterns for intricate embroidery and then she would execute her designs into beautiful works of art. She knitted large wall hangings with Native American patterns, all of her own design, and was also a fantastic cook. Keeping a beautiful garden, she would take Mary to the countryside to collect wild flowers. Together they would plant these wild flowers in the garden directly across from the rose flower bed. Her prized roses were of many different shades, from white to slightly darker and all the way to the darkest red. Mary's father was the opposite of her mother. According to Mary, "He was very bookish, retiring, and a quiet kind of man." He worked at Otto Zimmerman Printing Company, which was a music printing company. Together, her parents wanted to raise a Victorian daughter; indeed, they wanted her hands to stay beautiful and thus would not allow her to play the zither or the mandolin.

As Mary's parents felt that Newport was a very insular place, they often shuttled Mary across the river to Cincinnati, which had a symphony orchestra and choral society, where they enjoyed the performances. The city also had a museum they visited frequently and a stock repertory company that performed plays. Mary enjoyed the plays so much that she would return to her neighborhood Park Avenue Elementary School full of new ideas. On Friday afternoons, she led her fellow students in recreating the plays that she had seen in Cincinnati for their teachers. Mary was very influenced by this small school and the personalized teaching. Her principal encouraged creative activities. If anyone had a poem, an idea for a dance, or the plays Mary recreated, they had an opportunity to stage their performance. The principal also showed Charlie Chaplin and Buster Keaton movies. Mary's elementary school was very nurturing and featured prominently in Mary's early life. Each day, she walked to school along streets lined with large, established trees. On her journey, she was met by her "little friend" Melva Brown, from the city's northern side, and they would walk together. As they walked, other school mates joined them on their trips to and from school.

In grade school, Mary was part of a group of very bright students who she described as "full of beans." Her classes were organized very much like an orchestra in which there was a first chair, a second chair, and so forth, based on each month's academic accomplishments. Mary's group consisted of six students of three girls and three boys. They walked to school together every day. Mary especially loved the canopy trees and the smells of the lilies, along with the sound of the trolleys. Mary loved growing up in Newport, part of the Old South with its gracious manners.

Of this group, Mary stayed in touch with her childhood friend Melva Brown for many years. As children, when either of them became discouraged, they would give each other a big hug of encouragement. Another one of these friends was Betty Jo, daughter of the city's mayor, who lived in a big mansion. One very fond memory Mary has from this time is a day that she and and some classmates crossed the street from the school and bought a carton of sauerkraut. Horrified, her teacher sent them to the principal's office. Instead of punishing the children, however, the principal sent them across the street to purchase more sauerkraut. The principal used this as a teaching tool; while the students and the principal ate the sauerkraut together, they had a German culture class in the principal's office.

There were various Christian churches, but the dominant religion in Newport was Baptist. Prejudice toward other religions and races was also evident in the city. Mary's father was Catholic, and there was as much prejudice against Catholic families as there was for the African Americans. According to Mary, living in such an isolated community, she and other children had never heard of the Jewish religion until she was in 5th grade, when a Jewish girl moved to Newport and enrolled in her school. To help the new child feel more comfortable, her teacher talked to the class about Jewish customs, traits, and matzo. The teacher held a matzo party to teach the students about the Jewish culture.

Like many children, Mary's favorite time of the year was Christmas. For her, it was the excitement, the family and cousins together, and the Christmas tree. Oddly, she wasn't really interested in the Christmas presents. She remembers that one Christmas morning, her cousins were opening their presents rapidly. Instead of opening her own presents, Mary was dancing around the Christmas tree. One could say that she was born with the spirit of dance. When her family had company, she would run underneath the dining room table laughing. She was tiny for her age and was short enough to stand beneath the table among the adults' legs.

When Mary was about five years old, she became ill for a long time. She was so ill, in fact, that she was bedridden for months. Mary never knew exactly what she had, but it was likely the Asian flu epidemic that passed through the country at that time. There was a point that she couldn't eat, and she was only able to drink distilled water for 10 long days. She still remembers the clink of the glass bottles by her bed. After her diet of distilled water, she was finally permitted to drink bouillon. Her first solid meal at that time was mashed potatoes, ground steak, and spinach, a meal she has never forgotten. Because of the illness, Mary was unable to start school with other children her age. As such, her mother taught her the entire alphabet and basic arithmetic.

At the time, the doctor told Mary's mother that Mary needed a reason to live, and he suggested dancing lessons. Her mother promptly enrolled her in a gymnasium in Newport, a German location for exercise with drilling, parallel bars, and equipment typically used in physical education. On the ground floor of this gymnasium was a swimming pool that had a strange dank smell that permeated the entire building. On the upper floor were the rings, parallel bars, and a volleyball court. Mary hated the drilling, and she always fell off of the parallel bars. But she enjoyed studying piano with Maude, the gymnasium's pianist. Mary's favorite activity at the gymnasium was folk dancing. It was here that Mary said "There was glimmer of the beginning of her love of dance."

With Mary enjoying the folk dancing, her mother enrolled her into ballet classes at one of those "dreadful tiny tot ballet schools" where they taught ballet, tap, and acrobatics all in the same hour. This particular school staged an annual recital at Christmas time instead of the end of the academic year. Her teacher gave her a solo called *Miss Lipstick* to perform in the recital. Her mother watched every one of the many rehearsals. On the night of the performance, the pianist accidentally played the wrong musical score. Hearing different music, Mary improvised a solo on the spot from beginning to end. Her teacher wasn't sure whether to be upset with Mary or not, but the audience couldn't tell that it wasn't the dance she had been taught and had rehearsed. Only her mother and her teacher knew.

During her elementary school days, Mary's parents took her to the opera *La Giodonda* in Cincinnati, where she saw "The Dance of the Hours." Her parents purchased the vinyl record of this music for her. She listened to that record on the phonograph and danced to her heart's content.

But as Mary got older, her parents didn't feel she was getting the education she needed, and they began to discuss Walnut Hills, a special school in Cincinnati. To be accepted to this school, a prospective student had to pass an exam and be a resident of Cincinnati. Mary passed the exam, and her parents enrolled her under her cousin's Cincinnati address. No one at Walnut Hills knew that Mary had to navigate two-and-a-half hours of street car transportation (involving three different street cars from Newport to Cincinnati) every morning and every evening of every day to go to school. This was one of the lies in Mary's life. And with this lie, Mary learned that the truth can be pulled and interpreted in many different directions. Unfortunately, Mary's parents forced her to go to Walnut Hills, and she was absolutely miserable. There were as many students in her grade alone as there had been in the whole of her Kentucky school. The good thing about this school, though, was that in her second year of the high school, Mary's physical education teacher piled the students into a bus, and they went to see Martha Graham perform. Martha Graham was revolutionary in dance. She broke away from classical ballet and created her own dance language, which audiences did not always appreciate in its beginnings, especially outside of New York. When Mary watched Martha, she was so moved and mesmerized that it didn't matter that half of the audience walked out during one of Martha's solos. During the concert, Martha did all solos with Louis Horst playing the piano. Mary said to herself, "That is for me!"

During the summers, Mary worked with her father in the music printing factory. On the weekends, Mary helped her grandmother (on her mother's side) with housework and cleaning. This grandmother was very hard on Mary; so hard, in fact, that her sweet gentle-natured grandfather told her to "lay off the child." Mary's grandfather worked in a brass foundry that made faucets. His hobby and love, though, was singing in the opera company whenever he had the opportunity.

Mary's mother was one of three girls. Edna lived in Cincinnati, and Cora lived on a farm in Indiana. Aunt Cora's farm was Mary's absolute favorite place to go. She has fond memories of her aunt putting on boiling water while her uncle went to pick fresh corn. The corn literally went from the garden to the boiling water to the table; and it tasted so good, as did the fresh tomatoes from the garden. The farm house was an old country home permeated with the special fragrance of the wood-burning fireplace.

During Mary's childhood, her mother rented out a room in their house to a young man whom Mary calls Mr. X. (Mary doesn't want to honor this man by using his real name.) This triangular situation and the secrecy that surrounded it was the biggest lie that Mary witnessed. Mr. X and Mary's mother were exceedingly close and grew more so as the years wore on. Mr. X even ate dinner with the family, having his own chair at the dining room table. Mary knew the truth and so did her father, but life in their house was as if nothing was going on. Mary had such mixed feelings about her mother. She loved her very much, but at the same time she resented her, and felt sorry for and a bit protective of her father. Mary's father was a sweet, dear man, who Mary adored. She would have done anything for him that she could.

Mr. X also ran the gymnasium in Newport where Mary's mother enrolled her when she was recovering from her illness. Mary has vivid memories of Mr. X teaching her classes, pounding his cane on the floor to keep the tempo of the marching rhythms. Her mother volunteered at the gymnasium to be close to Mr. X; together they even wrote the newsletter for the gymnasium.

As a member of the Rotary Club, Mr. X invited his Rotarian friends to dinner three days per week at the gymnasium, and Mary's mother cooked for these dinners. Mary and her mother served approximately 18 men of the Rotary Club for each meal. After dinner, Mary's father picked Mary up, while her mother stayed behind. Mary and her father would then go to the movies. Her favorite movie actress was Billie Dove. After the movies, Mary and her father typically come home to an empty house. Each of these nights, Mary stayed awake until she heard the footsteps of her mother and Mr. X returning home very late. One particular summer, Mr. X and Mary's mother went to Europe for several weeks, and Mary decided she couldn't stand this situation any longer. She begged her father to leave her mother. His reply was always the same; that he couldn't leave her. He loved her mother too much.

Following graduation from high school, Mr. X convinced Mary's parents that she needed to enroll at the University of Cincinnati as a physical education major. This part of Mary's life became an additional lie. Embarking on a college education, Mary wasn't sure what she wanted to do with her life, but she knew in her heart that she did not respect Mr. X or his recommendations. Unfortunately, she was not emotionally strong enough to say how she really felt. During her first year as a physical education major, she worked for the English department. Hating physical education and loving English, Mary changed her major to English at the end of that first year.

Mary's home life became unbearable. After she completed her second year at the university, her father told Mary he was going to kill Mr. X; he had finally had enough. So, too, had Mary. During her first two years in college, the lie, the secrecy of her mother and Mr. X, and watching her father suffer, had to end for Mary. She was building up the courage to leave home for good. During this time, she composed a letter, which she kept in her desk drawer for the day she would "run away." When she could take no more, Mary mailed the letter, left home, and took the train to New York City.

From a 1965 issue of *Dance Magazine*, author Josephine Fox summed up Mary's childhood experience in her article "The Day is Mine, the Land is Mine."

> There was an aspect of my childhood that set me apart from other people and made me a loner. I grew up under a roof that was shared by my mother, my father, and another man. A little girl can sense a lot. And I knew I couldn't bring friends home. I knew my home wasn't quite my own. But I learned to escape…

Mary Anthony at 6 months

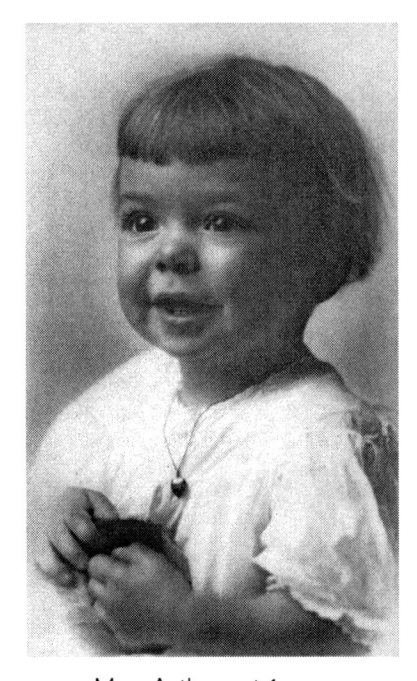

Mary Anthony at 1 year

Mary Anthony at 1 year

Mary Anthony at 2-3 years

Mary Anthony's mother

Mary Anthony's mother

Mary Anthony's mother

Mary Anthony's father

Mary Anthony's father as a boy

Mary Anthony's father

Mary Anthony's 1st grade, Park Elementary School in Newport, Kentucky, Mary is in the 2nd row, 2nd from the left

Mary Anthony at 9 years

Mary's grandmother on her mother's side

Mary's grandfather on her mother's side

The Daughters: Edna, Cora, Linda

From left to right, Aunt Edna, Aunt Cora and Mary's mom Linda

Mary's great grandmother (Mary's mother's mother)

A Dancer's Journey "It All Started With A Lie" 15

Julia Brennan, Mary's great grandmother on her father's side

Mary's high school graduation photo

Mary's high school graduation photo

CHAPTER 2

The Hanya Holm Years

With a whirlwind of emotions, Mary cried the entire trip to New York. It was difficult to leave home and scary to move to another place with the little money she had saved in her piggy bank. Because of Mary's interest in the arts, she chose New York City as the place to go. To her, it seemed that all the best talent came from New York. On the eastbound train, a young sailor observed Mary's sadness. Being a gentleman, he was worried about her safety. Here she was, leaving a small town all alone to move to a big city. Furthermore, she had not made any plans about where she would live when she arrived. The sailor recommended the Young Men and Young Women's Hebrew Association, and he even escorted her there. During his short time in New York before going off to sea, he visited her every day and encouraged her to search for a job. He recommended that she go to an employment agency. Taking his advice, she found a job with the Child Education Foundation, pulling medical records for doctors.

Mary worked at the Foundation during that first year. Her interest in theater and literature attracted the attention of Mrs. Schwiebert who worked at the Foundation. She recommended that Mary finish her education and encouraged her go to Vassar College, where Hallie Flanagan,[2)] a well-reputed teacher, was heading the drama department. Mrs. Schwiebert helped Mary win an academic scholarship to Vassar. Unfortunately, Mary didn't have the money for room and board, so she had to decline the scholarship. Mary also became friends with Dr. Stubbs, a female psychologist, who also worked at the Foundation. Dr. Stubbs told her that Hallie Flanagan graduated from Grinnell College in Iowa and urged Mary to look at the school. Subsequently, Dr. Stubbs gave Mary a ride to Grinnell when she was going home to Iowa. After a year on her own, Mary left New York City to attend Grinnell College. Here she earned her Bachelor's degree in theater. Mary loved dancing and had wanted to pursue that as well, but dance wasn't offered at Grinnell. Finishing college in 1940, Mary returned to New York to become an actress.

Mary knew a fellow Grinnell graduate who had already moved to New York. He was living in a boarding house and invited Mary to stay in his room for her first few weeks, as he was away on vacation. The rooming house was on 211 West 11th Street, and the landlady was Gretchen Schaefer. At that time, every room in the house was empty except the young man's. After Mary's friend returned, Ms. Schaefer offered Mary one of the other rooms in the house. In lieu of rent, Mary showed rooms to potential lodgers and answered the telephone. The arrangement also included meals, because Mary agreed to clean as well. For Mary, this was a perfect situation. During her stay, she lived in every room in the house, including the kitchen if all the rooms were filled. While Mary washed the windows and cleaned, Ms. Schaefer allowed Mary to play her Brahms, Bach, and Beethoven on the phonograph.

On occasion, Ms. Schaefer stayed on Long Island for a week or so. During her absence, Mary made space available to her friends who were moving to New York City with aspirations of becoming playwrights, costume designers, or other theater positions. Mary enjoyed those times when the landlord was gone, as she and her friends spent long hours talking at the dining room table while eating hamburger dinners. Of course, when the landlady returned from Long Island, her friends had to find another place to stay.

Soon Mary realized that getting a theater job wasn't necessarily about her acting ability, but more about the "casting couch." Because that made becoming an actress undesirable, she began looking at other professions in the arts. Mary's other love was dance, so she decided to look for opportunities. A scholarship was a must for her to afford dance training. She first went to the Martha Graham School, where she learned that the scholarships were only awarded to the men. Next, she went to the Humphrey Weidman Dance studio. As the company was out on tour, Mary met Nona Shurman, who was working there. Mary explained she would wash windows and scrub floors—do anything—for a dance scholarship. She only had $25 and desperately needed a working scholarship. A week later, when the company returned from tour, Pauline Lawrence, the company's manager and secretary, called Mary and asked to meet her in person. Very excited, Mary ran to the studio only to learn that Pauline just wanted see for herself the girl who came with only $25 and no previous dance training, with the hope of becoming a dancer. In retrospect, Mary does not feel that Pauline was being cruel, but that she really just wanted to meet the kid who came to New York with no money and stars in her eyes wanting to be a dancer.

Disappointed, tears ran down Mary's cheeks. Charles Weidman, co-studio owner with Doris Humphrey, had observed the entire conversation. He introduced himself and instructed Mary to go to Hanya Holm, who had left Germany for America to set up a dance school in the Mary Wigman technique. Fortunately for Mary Anthony, Hanya Holm was holding scholarship auditions the very next week; the winner of the scholarship would get three years of dance training.

When Mary arrived at the Hanya Holm audition, she was taken aback by the dancers who were warming up with exercises that Mary had never seen. These dancers had spent many years in the study of modern dance. Already instruments of dance, these beautiful athletes were intimidating to Mary, who had little to no dance training. Mary just had dreams. Overcome by fear and inadequacy, Mary decided to leave. Just as she was about to turn away, a young dancer and dance critic, Hy Glickman, encouraged her to stay. He said she had as good a chance as anyone else. His philosophy, which is an excellent philosophy for anyone with a dream, was "to try." It is better to try and fail, than to never have tried at all.

With the hopeful dancers gathered together, the formal audition began. Brought into the lovely studio from the waiting area, Mary saw all of the judges lined up, sitting in chairs with their papers and pencils, ready to scrutinize them. The judges were Hanya Holm, Louise Kloepper, and the eight members of the School's Board of Directors.

The audition was divided into three parts. The first part focused on technique. The dancers were given center floor exercises consisting of pliés, tendus ("brushes" is the modern dance term), degagés, adagio work, and grand battements to jumps. As Mary didn't know what a plié was, she just followed everyone else. The judges were watching to see the level of technique each dancer possessed, but most importantly, they were watching whether the dancers performed the exercises exactly the way the rehearsal mistress had shown. Dancers need to be instruments for the choreographers, and they need to replicate each and every movement with the mood and expression expected of them. Moving across the floor is important, as well. It reveals the dancer's use of space with movement. Mary was like an open tablet waiting for the words to be written. Although she lacked technique, Mary had an open mind to watch and listen to the instructions that were presented. Giving each move her most, she danced each stream of steps with guts, will, and passion. At this point, she didn't have anything to lose.

The second part of the audition included presenting two solos. The dancers were required to bring in two 78 rpm vinyl records for their individual solos. Mary did her first solo to the only record she had, "Clair de Lune." Because she only had the one record, she had no choice but to do her second solo in silence. With her background in literature and religion, combined with her sense of theater, Mary performed her solo on the theme of Adam. Music had been the inspiration for most modern dance to this point, so the thought of dancing in silence was unique. The judges, especially Hanya, were excited and impressed.

The third part of the audition was improvisation. Mary had thrown herself into this Holm audition with everything she had. She danced the improvisation section with full and free abandon. Mary knew that her chance for a scholarship award was doubtful, but she still held out hope.

During the entire week following the audition, Mary was on pins and needles. Each day when the postman came to the door, she was afraid and excited at the same time. Finally, the postman delivered the long-anticipated letter. To Mary's amazement, she was awarded the only three-year Hanya Holm dance scholarship. With excited shock, she read the letter over and over. She thought maybe her lack of training had helped her. When dancers have trained many years with a certain style, they resist changing to another way of moving. Or if the dancer was trained improperly, it is more difficult to remove bad habits and retrain. Even today, Mary believes that perhaps it was easier to teach someone so green. Now, Mary would have to work hard to show Hanya that she deserved the scholarship and prove that she could make it through the probationary period.

With tremendous enthusiasm Mary began her studies with Hanya Holm in 1940. Mary's first impression of Hanya was of her tiny face with piercing blue eyes and her strict expression as she choreographed and taught. Originally, the Hanya Holm School in New York City was the Mary Wigman Satellite School in the United States. In Europe, Mary Wigman was a German dance pioneer. On one of the Wigman tours, Sol Hurock, a legendary impresario who represented and managed many artists and companies, saw the company perform and wanted to bring the Wigman technique to the United States dance capital—New York City. Mary Wigman had to choose one of her most esteemed and trusted dancers for this endeavor, and she chose Hanya Holm. The Mary Wigman School opened in New York City in 1931. The school ran very successfully until 1936, when the anti-Nazi movement influenced Americans against the German culture and its people. This made it impossible to operate a school under the German name of Mary Wigman in the United States. Hanya contacted Mary Wigman and expressed this complicated dilemma, as it was affecting her enrollment and funding. Mary Wigman suggested removing the Wigman name and renaming it the Hanya Holm School of Dance. Holm didn't have a German-sounding name.

Hanya had been at the helm of the school for nine years before Mary Anthony earned her scholarship to study there. For the last four of those years, the school had been in Hanya's name. Thus, by 1940, Hanya Holm was quite established in New York City. The Hanya Holm School had classes all day long and well into the evening hours. Classes included dance technique, percussion, Labanotation, choreography, and improvisation. In this rich environment, Mary learned how to explore movement. "What a wonderful place to learn, study and rehearse," she said.

In those early days of Mary's study, Louise Kloepper, a Holm dancer and teacher, taught most of the Holm technique classes. She was an exceptional, inspiring teacher, and Mary adored and looked up to her. Louise Kloepper had received her earliest training in Seattle with ballet teacher

Mary Ann Wells. After graduating from high school, Louise moved to Germany to study with Mary Wigman. She was the first American dancer to complete the Wigman course, which included dance theory, percussion, dance technique, and group dances. Hanya Holm was one of the instructors in the original Mary Wigman School in Germany. After Hanya Holm came to the United States to run the New York based Mary Wigman School, she invited Louise to teach there.

The classes Hanya taught were mostly improvisation classes, which were held every Friday. Dancers were given specific directives to explore a particular style of expression and form that Hanya brought with her from Germany. From a young age, Hanya studied music and later graduated from the Institute of Emile Jacques-Dalcroze in Germany. There she innovated a unique way to work with music. She developed what is called "music visualization." According to Walter Sorell in *Hanya Holm, the Biography of an Artist*, "Dalcroze demanded that what she learned musically, she must also express physically. In other words, she was asked to do improvisations to rhythmic or musical themes."[3] The Hanya Holm School had a spacious dance studio with high ceilings that also included an outside garden. At Christmas time, Hanya transformed the studio into a European Christmas wonder. The high ceilings were hung with wreaths, and the Christmas tree was adorned with candles. At that time in the state of New York, candles on Christmas trees were outlawed because of the danger of fire. So, before lighting the candles, Hanya closed the blinds so that no one could see from the outside in. For these Christmas celebrations, Hanya cooked and served a German menu for the dancers, which consisted of mulled wine and black bean soup to warm the heart. Mary Anthony's first Christmas party at the studio was the most glorious party she had ever attended. And, what made it even more special was that Hanya patted Mary on the head and told her that her probationary period was over. Mary Anthony was now a real part of the school.

In 1941, during Mary's first year as a student, Hanya choreographed *The Golden Fleece* with music by Alex North, and the costumes, sets, and ideas were created by the surrealistic designer, Kurt Seligman. For Mary, this was a wonderful time to see Hanya at work with her dancers. Unfortunately, this particular piece of choreography had several problems. Walter Terry, critic for the New York *Herald Tribune* and *Saturday Review*, dismissed this work with the remark that "...the costumes of Kurt Seligmann were fantastic to an extreme but that the dancing failed to match their inventiveness and was much too delicate and noncommittal instead of being equally strong and grotesque." Even John Martin, dance critic for the New York *Times* and author of several books, had taken time to observe some rehearsals before reviewing the opening night. He had seen the choreography without costumes in rehearsal, and then later saw the big cumbersome costumes on stage. For example, the Phoenix costume was long, heavily draped fabric with a huge mask. Martin felt the costumes and masks monopolized the work and made the movement secondary to the costumes. Because the costumes hindered the movement, the company members became very frustrated. The dancers felt they could not perform the choreography that Hanya had established for them. Hanya's frustration stemmed from the fact that the dancers did not have the costumes to work in until the first performance. By that point, it was too late to change any of her choreography. Louise Kloepper played the part of the Phoenix. As a bird, Louise performed pecking movements that Hanya had choreographed for her. During the performance, when she finally put on the costume and the heavy mask, she fell forward onto her face. To make things worse, the masks limited the dancers' vision.

With the bad reviews and the dancers' frustration, the entire company left Hanya except for Louise Kloepper, who was dedicated to Hanya. On several occasions Martha Graham had tried to hire Louise, but she remained loyal. With the departure of so many company members, Hanya was forced to use her dance students to create her new company, along with Louise Kloepper. Her dance students were not really ready to become part of the dance company, however. In the past, to become a company member in the Hanya Holm Company, a dance student had to not only achieve the advanced level of technique, but also had to apprentice with the company for two or three years beyond mastering technique. Only then were the dancers ready to perform Hanya's work on a professional level.

For Mary Anthony, this was a great break, after only having studied with Hanya for a single year. Imagine her excitement and trepidation all at the same time! The official date Mary joined the Hanya Holm Company was January 16, 1943, and a year thereafter, Mary became Hanya's personal assistant. She continued working with Hanya until 1949.

Later, Louise Kloepper also left Hanya, but for different reasons than the previous company members. Although Louise was a gorgeous and artistic dancer, she had terrible stage fright. She would become physically ill when she had to perform. Thus, she made a career change and became a teacher. She attended the University of Wisconsin, where she worked and studied dance with Margaret Doubler. After graduating, Louise became an assistant professor at that same university and later become the department's chairperson for dance.[4]

After Louise left for the university, Hanya asked Mary an important question.

"Mary, do we close the studio, or do we stay open?"

"Hanya, that depends upon you," Mary answered.

"We stay open!" was Hanya's enthusiastic response.

At this point, Mary began teaching at Hanya's school, managing all the classes except the advanced class. Mary didn't really feel ready to teach, but Hanya assured her that she was ready. At that time, the school had only two advanced students: Mary Anthony and Molly Howe. Hanya taught this advanced class of two as if it were a class of 20 students. From Hanya, Mary learned that even if there is a snowstorm, and only two students come to class, you teach the class as if it were a full class. By taking Hanya's classes, Mary learned how to structure her own classes.

There were many components to the Hanya Holm School. Each day, the dancers would not only take technique class and learn choreography, but also participate in an assortment of other classes. These classes helped mold Mary into what she would become. In her first year at the school, Mary was in the pedagogy class that Hanya taught. As part of this class, Hanya had the students teach. After this assignment, Hanya evaluated their work. Was the work on the floor too long? Were they prepared to jump or had they spent too much time on the diagonal? Hanya was a great pedagogy teacher, who really made her students think. Mary calls Hanya "the teacher's teacher." She felt Hanya was more of a teacher who taught aspiring dance teachers than a technique teacher for the dancers.

Also, in Mary's first year, Hanya would schedule private classes with her students. During Mary's very first private class with Hanya, they covered the plié, which Mary thought she already knew. To Mary's amazement, Hanya spent an hour and a half going into depth, quality, and purpose for pliés. Each private lesson with Hanya featured this specialized and meticulous work.

During the company rehearsals, scholarship students and apprentices were expected to sit on the floor all afternoon and observe the company rehearse. At the same time, they had to learn the choreography of each dancer. If any of the company members were absent from rehearsal, the apprentice dancers were expected to know and be able to fill the part, when requested, even though they had been just sitting and observing. This was great training for these young dancers. It forced the apprentices to focus and really learn the choreography.

Before Mary got into the Holm Company, she was required to take company class every day at 4 PM. Although Mary wasn't ready technically, this was an invaluable experience. Hanya didn't care if a dancer did the movement perfectly. She just wanted the dancer to try. This approach trained Mary to learn quickly. At the Hanya Holm studio, dancers took classes from noon until 8 or 9 PM. That left the morning free to undertake work to earn money to live. The free mornings provided Mary with the time to work at the boarding house, cleaning, answering the phone, and showing rooms.

During this time with Hanya, Mary had the opportunity to study percussion from one of the greatest musicians and composers, Henry Cowell. On February 7, 1943, she performed with the renowned John Cage, a previous student of Henry Cowell, who was a pioneer in avant-garde music, along with Xenia Cage and dancer Merce Cunningham and others. The performance took place at the New York Museum of Modern Art. During this special experience, Mary was playing percussion as part of the orchestra; indeed, such music education was invaluable. Furthering her music studies, she also studied piano with Norman Lloyd. Hanya's school provided for such a well-rounded education.[5]

The students and apprentices also learned repertory that had already been performed previously. Two of these works were *Trend* and *Tragic Exodus*, which called for a large dance company of dancers. Originally, Hanya had choreographed the very successful work called *Trend* at Bennington College, which held large summer dance festivals each summer.

Every summer starting in 1941, Hanya also taught at Colorado State College in Colorado Springs, Colorado. There, she founded the Colorado College Summer School of Dance. This school afforded her the opportunity to experiment with new choreography, as she brought her company members along with her. She would also use select students in the performance, giving them a chance to learn through performing. One summer, Hanya choreographed a work called *Orestes and the Furies*. In this work, Mary performed as Apollo. For the Colorado performance, Arch Lauterer was the scene designer. He built a fascinating set that featured a long ramp for Apollo that extended up from the stage and out the back of the theater to the lawn outside. With the ramp painted black and the lighting effects, it appeared as if Apollo was descending from the sky as Mary ran down the ramp and leapt onto the stage. The Colorado costume designer put the furies in earth tones with tights that combined green, brown, and dark red. Such colors enhanced the dancers' movements.

The Colorado performance of *Orestes and the Furies* took place on August 14, 1943. It was received with great success, unlike its New York premiere, which was performed later. In New York, Hanya did not have the financial resources to stage the work the way she had done in Colorado. She could not afford the sets that Arch Lauterer had made, and she had a different costume designer. The New York costume designer made the costumes for the Furies a shocking pink. Mary remembers that the New York audience laughed at the Furies as they entered the stage on their first entrance. Edwin Denby, in his book *Looking at the Dance**, speaks of the entire work. He said, "It looked to me like a graduation event put on by the girls' physical education department; posture work, intermediate and advanced, neatly and seriously performed." In Denby's book *Dance Writings* on page 197 (Alfred A. Knopf), he says "The trouble with Miss Holm's desire to arrange her pedagogic material in the form of a story. It led, as stories will, to groupings on the floor that presented the young ladies from rather awkward angles." He continued, "However, when all these girls galloped friskily across the stage the effect was jolly, and the audience laughed happily, Furies or no Furies."[6] He gave Hanya a damaging review of this New York performance in the New York *Herald Tribune* on January 30, 1944.[7] Hanya was very upset with the review, and when Mary tried to console her, Hanya only grew more angry. Another work for which Hanya received bad reviews was a work called *Namesake*, which was based on *The Spoon River Anthology*.

During this time in New York dance history, there were three major modern dance schools in New York: Martha Graham, Humphrey-Weidman, and Hanya Holm. Dancers came to one of these studios to become professional concert dancers. Students, however, did not studio-hop. They were devoted to one style, and these same concert dancers would never think of dancing on Broadway. "We were too pure for that," Mary said. Furthermore, Graham dancers didn't talk to Holm dancers and so forth.

Among the American women who had a definite impact on modern dance in the first half of the 20th century, three stood out: Helen Tamiris, Martha Graham, and Doris Humphrey. Although Helen Tamiris was outspoken and strong-willed, according to Mary, " she was really sweet." That sweetness filtered down to the dancers who worked for her. They, in turn, were open to mingling with other groups of dancers, when modern dancers of the time socialized only with the dancers from their own school. Mary Anthony particularly loved working for Helen.

Hanya lived her life in the context of having survived World War I in Germany, where food was scarce, and the lifestyle was strict and severe. According to Mary, while in Germany, Hanya only ate turnips for two years and endured many hardships. Her survival mode became very evident when a dancer might ask Hanya to be absent from a class or rehearsal for any reason. One time, Mary was suffering with an impacted wisdom tooth that had to be extracted. Mary arrived at the studio with her mouth filled with cotton to stop the bleeding. Mary asked Hanya if she could be excused from teaching that afternoon. Hanya, in her German accent, asked "Vy?" Subsequently, Mary taught her class with her mouth full of cotton. Mary also learned that for Hanya in Germany, there was no anesthesia when a tooth was pulled. She also learned to teach her class no matter the circumstances.

Later, Mary learned that during World War I in Germany, the Mary Wigman dancers traveled in box cars, from venue to venue, painting china to sell. This was necessary for the dancers to have enough money to pay for their dance concerts on tour. The Wigman dancers were literally paying their way for an opportunity to dance. Staying warm was another challenge. At that time, it was cold in the theaters and studios. As such, the dancers had to warm up in their goulashes and coats, and as they slowly warmed up their bodies, they would peel off these outer layers.

After Mary had been working and teaching at Hanya's studio, Glen Tetley appeared at the studio dressed in his sailor uniform, having just been discharged from the military. He asked if he could train there. Hanya's studio began growing; at the same time, ballet dancers from New York City Ballet and American Ballet Theatre began to realize they needed to study modern dance as well as ballet. This was because modern choreographers were being hired to choreograph for ballet companies. The dancers who came from American Ballet Theatre to study with Hanya were Annabelle Lyon, Bambi Linn, Ray Harrison, and Rod Alexander. The classes were filled with these beautifully ballet trained dancers who needed more expression and new ways to move.

By this time, Mary had become an esteemed dancer for Hanya. Hanya would experiment on Mary, as they shared a common language in the Holm technique. After Glen had been training at the studio for a while, Hanya would work with them together. When Hanya choreographed *Ozark Mountain Suite*, she relied on Mary and Glen, as they would improvise for her with given directions. After they learned what Hanya wanted, they would, in turn, teach the choreography to the other dancers. *Ozark Mountain Suite* was a huge success. The work was performed on May 29, 1947 at Needles Trades and on December 20, 1947 at Brooklyn Academy of Music.

By this time, other choreographers were also noting Mary's dancing. Sophie Maslow asked Mary to be in her choreography of *Folksay*. To do this, Mary had to ask Hanya's permission; Hanya agreed, as long as it didn't interfere with Mary's teaching obligations at the studio. Sophie Maslow, Jane Dudley, Bill Bales, and Mary performed in *Folksay*. After dancing in some of Hanya's recent pieces that had received poor reviews, it was gratifying for Mary to dance in such a successful work. Mary loved Sophie's choreography—and hearing the response of an audience who enjoyed it.

During the time that Mary danced for Hanya, she learned life lessons in addition to dance. Through all of Hanya's ups and downs, she came to know her exceptionally well. Hanya was an enormous disciplinarian. In remembering Hanya, Mary is inspired by her strength. She survived the war and kept dancing while living and growing in this adversity. For example, before Hanya left Germany, she had given birth to a son whose father was a painter/sculptor named Reinhold Martin Kuntze. When he learned Hanya was pregnant, he left her. After her son's birth, Hanya brought her baby son Klaus to the Wigman studio in a basket.

When teaching class or conducting rehearsals in the 60s and 70s, Mary often speaks of how the times were so different back when she was training with Hanya Holm. Dancers rehearsed without compensation. And, they were lucky to receive $5 for a performance. Dancers were happy to dance; indeed, earning a living was secondary.

The year 1948 was a turning point for Hanya. Unfortunately, Hanya had to release her company of many years due to growing financial difficulties. At this point Hanya began choreographing for Broadway. She continued to choreograph modern dance concerts, but mostly for the Colorado Springs summer students. During her introduction to Broadway, Hanya was asked by Jose Ferrer if she would be interested in choreographing *The Insect Comedy*, a Czechoslovakian play with a great deal of movement. Hanya, feeling insecure about this endeavor, asked Mary what she thought. Mary assured Hanya that she would be perfect for the job, as she was gifted in moving any size group of dancers or actors around in an assortment of patterns. Additionally, earlier in 1948, Hanya received an offer to choreograph *Ballet Ballads* on Broadway. Hanya Holm later choreographed several big Broadway musicals including *Kiss Me Kate*, *Camelot*, and *My Fair Lady*, among others.

Mary Anthony, photo for Hanya Holm 1947

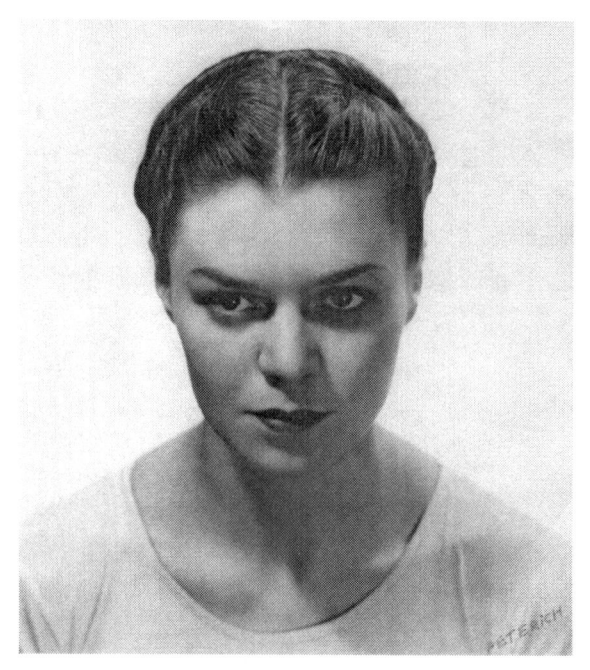

Mary Anthony, 1945 photo taken for Hanya Holm concert season, photo by Gerda Peterich

Mary Anthony performing in John Cage's Percussion Concert
at the Museum of Modern Art on February 7, 1953

"Ozark Mountain Suite", choreographed by Hanya Holm, left to right - Annabelle Lyon
with Ray Harrison, Mary Anthony with Glen Tetley, and Bambi Linn with Oliver Kostock,
photo by Thomas Bouchard

"Ozark Mountain Suite", choreographed by Hanya Holm,
from left to right - Mary Anthony with Glen Tetley, Annabelle Lyon
with Ray Harrison, and Bambi Linn with Oliver Kostock

CHAPTER 3

A Bird Must Fly Away

For most dancers of the 1940s to make a living, it was necessary to teach, perform, and take on a variety of jobs all at the same time. Mary Anthony's life became very rich once she was trained to dance and to teach. And, her life was full of adventures in every respect.

By the time Hanya was back on her feet financially with her first Broadway hit *Kiss Me Kate* and having dissolved her New York based company around 1948, Mary thought it was time to leave and do her own work. Plus, Alwin Nikolais had started training at the studio and seemed like the perfect person to fill the void that Mary would leave. Years before, Alwin had seen a Mary Wigman performance and was inspired to dance. He attended Bennington College, where he studied with Hanya Holm and others until his training was interrupted for several years to serve in the United States Army in World War II. Following his military service, Alwin returned to New York to study directly with Hanya Holm. There, he studied with both Mary and Hanya. Now with Alwin at the studio, Mary could envision the possibility of teaching less for Hanya.

Having done some outside work with other choreographers, Mary was feeling the need to branch out. Mary subsequently asked Hanya if she could possibly teach less. Just as quickly, she added that Nikolais wanted to begin to teach. Hanya's response: "Absolutely not!" Mary felt it necessary, therefore, to write a formal letter of resignation. It was not that she wasn't grateful for all that Hanya had done for her. Mary knew full well that her dance training and performing resulted from working with Hanya. Mary also knew that the scholarship award, together with Hanya's teaching, had allowed her to become a professional dancer and teacher. Later, after the dust had settled regarding Mary's decision to move on, Hanya said to Mary, "Well, one never wants to see a baby bird fly away; I know why they have to fly away, but I just did not want you to fly away."

During the time that Mary studied and worked for Hanya Holm, Mary earned her income by working in the mornings for the boarding house. One of Mary's jobs for the boarding house was to find renters. When the boarding house was full, the landlady, Gretchen Schaefer, would cook two special dinners each week for the residents. As she had done for the Rotary Club dinners when she was a child, one of Mary's duties was to serve the meals. Drinks were served at these dinners, and for the first time, Mary had a martini. She loved it!

Mary made friends with many of the residents of the boarding house. One of the boarding house renters was named Isabelle Lunbert, who had been married to a writer named Hearst. Isabelle painted the walls in her room purple with gold trim. Like her colorful room, she was a colorful person, who had a great influence on Mary. Ever encouraging of Mary's dancing, Isabelle and Mary became lifelong friends. Another boarder was named Bernard Hollander, who was a lawyer.

One night, Mary came home late from rehearsal, but the landlady, thinking Mary was out doing things that a young lady should not do, had locked the house. This left Mary with no choice but to walk the streets of New York City until the morning. After this happenstance, Mary decided to move from the boarding house. She only moved a block away to another home on 11th Street, where Richard Price lived. Richard was a poet who introduced Mary to the love and beauty of poetry. In Mary's earlier years, she had read Whitman and Longfellow, but Richard introduced her to other poets, such as e. e. cummings and Wallace Stevens. Many times, Mary and Richard would walk together and sit on the dock and read poetry on the corner of Hudson and 12th Street, where it extends into the Hudson River.

Another of the many small jobs Mary took to support herself was posing for artists. This began when Hanya's secretary suggested that she should start posing for extra money, which was a common job for dancers at the time. The secretary told Mary that when she received a call from someone who needed a dancer to pose, she would let her know. Mary remembers the first time she was actually hired. As promised, the secretary told her that an artist needed a model, but he wanted a nude model. Naturally, Mary was terrified. The secretary responded with "How dare you get on your high horse!" As Mary's small town religious upbringing was a large contrast to as large city like New York where the secretary grew up in. With trepidation, Mary called the artist for her first posing appointment.

Fortunately for Mary, the very first man for whom she posed was a sculptor named Allen Townsend Terrell. Ironically, he happened to be a very good friend of Gretchen ….. the German landlady in the boarding house on 11th Street where Mary had lived and worked. He gave Mary some very good advice about nude modeling, for which she always thanked him. He said, "If you keep your robe on until you step on the platform, and then take off your robe, we look at you as though we are looking at a piece of sculpture or a vase or some abstract figure. Then, be sure and put your robe back on before you step down from the platform." He said that models get into trouble if they walk around the room with no clothes on before or after posing. Mary posed for this man for two years, and during this time they established a long-lasting friendship.

Each morning when she arrived to work, Allen would say casually, "Oh, I haven't had my breakfast today and hate having breakfast alone." Or, when she would finish posing, he would say, "I just happened to make a casserole, and I hate having lunch alone." As money was scarce, Mary delighted in these meal invitations, which kept her nourished and gave her energy to dance. Mary also posed for the artists Raphael Soyer and William Zorach.

In 1944, Mary danced in the musical *Stovepipe Hat*, choreographed by Helen Tamiris, in Boston. Mary absolutely loved working for Helen, as she was a warm person with blonde curls and blue eyes. Tamiris was one of the choreographers that used African-American dancers at a time when most did not.

Dancers, like actors and authors, frequently changed their names. Helen's real name was Helen Becker (another example is Daniel Nagrin who was originally Danny Switch). Helen changed her last name from Becker to Tamaris because she admired the brave and gorgeous queen of Persia, who was ruthless and had the ambition to overcome all obstacles. Helen wished to emulate the queen's qualities. The daughter of Russian-Jewish immigrants, Helen grew up in New York City. In her youth, she studied "Interpretative Dancing from Irene Lewisohn and Blanche Talmud, and by fifteen years of age, she became a member of the Metropolitan Opera Ballet."[8] Later, Helen rebelled from ballet and Duncan-style dancing to discover and be herself. In her quest, she became involved in and later the director of the Dance Project for the Works Progress Administration (WPA), which resulted from an act of Congress, after so many suffered from the high unemployment rate during the depression. The WPA provided job opportunities for all kinds of workers. Jack Anderson, in his book *Art Without Boundaries – The World of Modern Dance*, wrote, "Actors, directors, stage designers, and dancers were assisted by WPA's Federal Theatre Project, formed in 1935 under the direction of Hallie Flanagan." Helen originally choreographed social protest against prejudice, poverty, racism, war, and suffering of mankind. As this movement faded, and she was dancing much less herself, she choreographed for Broadway.

Stovepipe Hat was one of those musicals in which the dancers were on stage for most of the performance with barely enough time to go offstage and change costumes. Although *Stovepipe Hat* was a story about the life of Abraham Lincoln, the character of Lincoln never actually appeared on the stage. The show was produced by Carl E. Ring at The Shubert Theater, with the book and lyrics by Walter F. Hannan, Edward Heyman, and Harold Spina, who also scored the music. The musical was directed by Robert Ross, and the costumes were designed by Lucinda Ballard. During the show's run, the producer made several changes to the show, and he became so entranced by the character of Abraham Lincoln that he even grew a long beard. One night, the dancers and cast members saw tears in the conductor's eyes. When the curtain came down, they learned that they had just completed their last performance. By making so many changes to the show without permission, the producer had violated his contract.

According to the New York *Times'* obituary of Carl E. Ring on Friday, June 14, 1991,

> In the late 1940s, [Ring] drew national attention with a Federal suit against the Dramatists Guild of the Authors League of America challenging a contract he had signed to produce *Stovepipe Hat*, a play about Abraham Lincoln. He sought to make changes in the play, but the authors refused, citing a contract provision that any changes required the author's approval. He repudiated the contract and closed the play, thus losing his standing with the Dramatists Guild. A jury ruled that the agreement violated the Sherman Antitrust Act but did not award damages, saying he had forfeited his right to relief by repudiating the contract and closing the play. In 1951, the United States Supreme Court refused to hear further arguments in the case.

A year later, in 1945, Mary met Joseph Gifford as they were rehearsing for the musical *Up in Central Park*, also choreographed by Helen Tamiris. *Up in Central Park* was based on the book by Herbert and Dorothy Fields (son and daughter of Lew Fields), with music by Sigmund Romberg and lyrics by Dorothy Fields. It was originally produced in1945 by Michael Todd and directed by John Kennedy. Both Mary and Joseph were replacing the two dance leads previously in the show. Joe remembers noting Mary for the first time at the rehearsals. When she wasn't actively rehearsing, she would read a book, but he interrupted her reading to introduce himself. Almost instantly, they became good friends. As they bonded, they discovered how much they had in common and that they shared similar dreams. During the show's run, Mary and Joe spent a lot of time together, dreaming of creating their own dance concert group. With the money they saved from this show, they were able to start to make their dream a reality.

Mary was offered teaching opportunities after leaving Hanya. Eve Gentry (whose real name was Henrietta Greenwood) was also a Hanya Holm company dancer and taught Labanotation at the Holm studio and teaching the Hanya Holm technique at The New Dance Group Studios. For years when she had a schedule conflict, she would have Mary substitute. June Dudley observed many of the classes Mary taught, and she invited Mary to join the faculty of The New Dance Group in 1946. Around this time, Hanya lost her beautiful studio on 11th Street that Mary knew and loved and had to move to another location on 8th Avenue.

The New Dance Group, started February 1932, was mostly second-generation American dancers in Hanya Holm's Wigman School. Their mission was to make dance a viable weapon for the struggles of the working class. The New Dance Group offered classes of every level to workers in order to combine recreation with art, and the members built a repertory of revolutionary dance pieces. Mostly modern dance, they included other forms of dance. The New Dance Group welcomed all races and religions. The organization continued with its ups and downs until 2009, when monies ran out and could no longer afford the exorbitant rent.

The New Dance Group had many styles of dance of which one could take advantage. Classes cost 5 cents each, but if you didn't have 5 cents, you could still take a class. There were several techniques taught. Jane Dudley and Sophie Maslow, who were referred to as Martha's titans, taught the Martha Graham technique. This is where Mary began her study of the Graham technique.

Later, Mary could financially afford to take a summer Graham course with Martha Graham. On the first day, Mary was in the elementary technique class, and on the second day she was placed in the intermediate class. By the third day, she had moved to the advanced class with Martha Graham herself teaching. When they performed the "knee exercise on six"—part of Graham's codified technique—Martha watched Mary closely, and she asked Mary to demonstrate the exercise. Terrified, Mary demonstrated the particular exercise, and Martha was impressed. Afterward, Martha asked "Where did you learn that?" Mary answered that she had learned the exercise from Jane Dudley, one of Martha's best dancers. Martha's reply was "I might have known!" Mary had many special memories of studying with Martha. Another memory comes from on one of the days in technique class when the class was doing triplets on the diagonal. Martha put her arm around Mary, and together they "tripleted," as Mary calls it, around the room. Martha exclaimed, "These are triplets!"

Mary really loved teaching at The New Dance Group. Each of her classes lasted one-and-a-half hours and was followed by a guided improvisation class. The classes met five days per week. Some of the students in Mary's class included Donald McKayle (who was 17 years old), Arthur Mitchell, John Fealy, Xavier Francis, Laura Sheleen, Doris Hering, Cordelia Ware, Esta Beck, Eve Beck (Esta and Eve were twins), Ronnie Aul, and Louis Mckenzie. Mary loved teaching these particular students and found them inspirational. Later, these same students branched out on their own. Xavier Francis eventually opened a school in Mexico, and Laura opened a school in Paris. Doris Herring became a dance critic for *Dance Magazine*. Another dancer, Cordelia Ware, went on to do the musical *The King and I*, and later married the actor George Hall.

When Donald McKayle auditioned for a scholarship at the New Dance Group, which he was awarded, Mary was on the judging panel. She was one of his first teachers, and one he remembers to this day. He said in an interview[9] with the author, "Mary was very light and alive, very defined, resourceful, and everything she taught in her class was carefully thought out." In fact, he admitted that Mary was his favorite teacher among all the teachers at The New Dance Group. Not only did Donald dance with Mary in *Blood Wedding* and *The Women of Troy*, but he also designed and made costumes for Mary. These costumes and designs are housed in the library of the University of California Irvine. One of Donald's favorite memories was going to Mary's apartment in Greenwich Village, where she made German potato salad, which he said was magnificent.

Board meetings at The New Dance Group were like big social gatherings rather than business meetings. Many of the members desired a larger performance venue, which inspired much of opposition within the group. The New Dance Group decided to hire the same producer, Peter Lawrence, who also produced for American Ballet Theatre. He secured the Ziegfield Theater for them in 1949, where Mary was featured very prominently. The performance included Mary Anthony, Joseph Gifford, Eva Desca, and Hadassah, who was a dance pioneer of Israeli and Indian dance.

In December 1946, Mary danced along with Jane Dudley, Sophie Maslow, and Bill Bales in the company they called the Dudley-Maslow-Bales Trio. She also danced the solo part in Anna Sokolow's *Lyric Suite*.

Fulfilling their dream of concert dancing, on May 6, 1947, Mary and Joseph Gifford danced together at the Brooklyn Museum in New York doing *The Pursued* and *The Unsleeping City*, both of which Gifford choreographed.

Besides Joseph Gifford, two people were encouraging Mary to start doing her own choreography: playwright Leslie Stevens and artist Kim Edgar Swados. Leslie Stevens was very good friends with Mary. He would encourage Mary to just go into the studio and work by herself, to spend several hours exploring movement. Not long thereafter, Mary and Joseph, who Mary affectionately calls Joe, choreographed a duet in which they each choreographed their own part. Mary went on to choreograph several solos. One of the solos was Lot's wife, taken from the Bible, titled *Genesis 19* to music by Stefan Wolpe. It was a story of daring to rebel. Mary's father was Catholic and her mother was Presbyterian. Actually, Mary liked her father's religion for the ritualistic theater that each mass contained. Biblical themes showed up in Mary's choreography frequently as she has read and reread the Bible cover to cover. Mary found her voice in choreography that told a story with a beginning, a middle, and an end. And, as Mary continued working on her own choreography, she gained confidence with each work.

On March 14, 1948, Mary and Joe Gifford performed with Katherine Litz at the 92nd Street Y. For this concert, Mary choreographed and performed *Lady Macbeth*, which was Mary's first full piece of choreography. It was a 13-minute solo with actors speaking and a set designed by a friend of Mary's. The concert included Mary's *Genesis 19* and *Chaconne* also to music by Stefan Wolpe. John Martin gave a glowing review of Katherine's work but hardly mentioned Mary and Joe at all. Upset with Martin's omission, Mary had the guts to write John directly. She explained to him that to get and secure touring, one needs good reviews. Mary went on to say how this could affect any possibility of touring, which is part of a dancer's livelihood. John wrote back to Mary, stating his opinion that it was really Katherine's Litz's evening. He felt that when Mary and Joe were more established, he would be happy to review them. Mary expressed that reviewers don't know how much power they possess. When a reviewer gives a glowing review, you can quote the review in your marketing packages, which makes it easier to obtain dates to perform. Mary commented on how difficult it is to get established before John would really review them.

According to Mary, reviewers had more power back then than they do today. The modern critics of her concert days were Walter Terry, John Martin, and Edwin Denby. John Martin wrote for the New York *Times*, and Walter Terry wrote for the *Herald Tribune*. The *Herald Tribune* wasn't considered as important as the *Times*. Even so, Mary loves Walter Terry as he writes the best and most informative reviews.

Mary drew from her vast literary background in choreographing her first work *Lady Macbeth*. She took two monologues from the famous Shakespeare play to portray the solo of Lady Macbeth. In the first section, she is costumed in a medieval gown. Her movements and gestures are strong, as she feels the throne is now finally her husband's, having convinced him to murder the previous king. Mary stayed on stage for the transition to the section where her maid helped her undress and change into a night gown. Given a white candle, Mary portrays the psychological agony of her hands stained with blood. With horrific guilt, she dances the infamous sleep walking scene, and dies in a fetal position by her candle.

Mary revisited this work on its 50th anniversary in 1999, and again in 2007, restaging it both times for company dancer Mary Ford. It was performed as part of the annual American Dance Guild Festival at the Hudson Guild Theater in the Chelsea neighborhood of New York City. Of the famous sleepwalking section of the solo in the 2007 review in the New York *Times*, Alastair Maculay wrote:

> Curiously, despite the racked and brooding nature of her thoughts here, the dance becomes less obsessive, not more; the main change is

in her loss of force. She places the candle on the floor, and it becomes one of her main points of focus. The solo ends, the dancer outstretched on the floor, with one last beseeching gesture toward the candle before she folds into death."[10]

The original music for *Lady Macbeth* was by Alfred Brooks. Unfortunately, the score was lost. She had to find new music, and in 1999, she used Arvo Pärt's *Fratres*. Mary actually like this new music, as she feels it works best with her choreography and staging.

A young dancer named Gwendolyn Jensen was present for this 2007 restaging of *Lady Macbeth* where she observed rehearsals and interviewed Mary Anthony. Inspired by Mary's use of literary themes found in Shakespeare and the Bible, she completed an in-depth study of Mary's work for her Master of Arts in Theatre and Dance thesis from the University of New Mexico in May 2010. Of *Lady Macbeth* she wrote,

> The set for the reconstruction consisted of considerably less than that for the 1949 version, as much of it was also lost after so many years. The original piece had an elaborate set with props, but this did not work well for touring so it was later minimized (Anthony). Anthony credits part of the dramatic inspiration in the piece to the fact that she was in a relationship with a playwright when she created it (Anthony). The following description is from Anthony's 1999 reconstruction of *Lady Macbeth* for Mary Ford, recorded in *Images and Reflections: Mary Anthony's Lady Macbeth*.
>
> Mary Ford as Lady Macbeth enters to alternate steadiness, shrillness, and silence in the music. Her arms are stretched forward and her focus is resolute as she enters. This action marks her reading of Macbeth's letter, which introduces her character in the play. Ambition and desire build along with effort as she strives steadily toward the throne, and sharp movement motifs carry her along the way. She executes attitude turns off-axis with her arms held open, shoulders raised, elbows slightly bent, and foot flexed. The tension and carriage of her body, along with her downward gaze, suggest a desired power that only a ruler can possess. Other movements include a sharp striking at her breasts and emotive gestures to the body. A motion toward the chest precedes a violently dismissive slicing of the arms away from each other and down toward the floor. Sharp gestures, including several separate moments of her tensely open hand with spread fingers behind her head, mirror accents in the music.
>
> Immediately after Lady Macbeth sits triumphantly on the throne, she begins to focus intently on her hands, with a sharp rubbing motion as though to get something off of them. Her body shudders as effort builds and her dancing becomes acute in its chaos and inward focus. Contractions and shaking reveal the effort and inner struggle of the infamously tragic character. Eccentric motions, such as

one hand gliding across her back to the other side of her body in a contorted fashion, mark the decline of any previous rationality as she sleepwalks across the floor holding a candle. Her inward focus becomes more tangible through a mad, glazed-over look in her eyes as she pauses between skitters across the floor or shudders in place, seeming to focus on the void in front of or above her. The dance winds down as Lady Macbeth's sanity slips further away from her. She slowly makes her way to the floor and finally collapses into stillness.

The dance uses space to define Lady Macbeth's intentions and her relationships to other characters and aspects of the play. In the beginning, Mary Ford focuses with forward intention as she moves toward the throne. Her eyes are piercing as she moves in strong motifs, revealing ambition and strength. She exudes confidence, which Ford shows in juxtaposition to the lack of clarity and focus of her facial expression in the sleepwalking scene. Ford shows a loss of purpose in her movement and she no longer clearly defines space with motivated pathways framing sharp gestures. She implies the presence of Macbeth through movement and focus, pausing in inquiry or disappointment, bowing in subservience, and reacting to betrayal with energetic confrontation. Ford also reveals her intentions with long, well-placed looks toward the empty throne on the opposite side of the stage. There are also moments in which she stares ahead, as though actually looking into another person's eyes to imply relationship and conversation.

In *Images and Reflections*, Anthony speaks of the emotional difficulty of *Lady Macbeth*, which adds to the physical difficulty of performing the movement. It requires a building of intensity and emotion before a peak and decline. Shakespeare's character declines from confident ambition into guilt with a mad, inward focus; both facets reflect the depth of the subject. The glazed-over look of the dancer during the sleep-walking scene of *Lady Macbeth* is important to the overall character and performance. Rather than putting on certain facial expressions, it is a natural continuation of the inner feeling which drives her movement and gestures. Anthony discusses this feeling and expression, saying that Al Pacino in the film *Scent of a Woman* showed a similar look as a blind character, reflecting the same inward focus or the loss of focus in madness. The expression of emotion in this dance is important for revealing the complexities of its subject.

Anthony similarly vocalizes the desire to portray Lady Macbeth's power as well as her beauty. The character must also be beautiful and feminine or Macbeth would not have married her (Anthony). Part of the difficulty of performing the character lies in the need to portray such a range of qualities; the character is ambitious and powerful while also remaining the delicate and beautiful woman that Macbeth married. Lady Macbeth's power in influencing Macbeth is this duality of fragile beauty and ambitious cunning. Anthony also says that her goal in her original creation and performance of *Lady Macbeth* was to encourage the audience to "go back and read Macbeth again, this time focusing on Lady Macbeth's character" (Anthony). In narrowing an entire play down to its one driving female character, Anthony drew attention to Lady Macbeth while also making a powerful statement for women.[11]

The New Dance Group had a festival of performances that took place on May 23-27, 1948. For this concert, Joseph Gifford choreographed: *The Pursued*, *Scherzo*, and *The Unsleeping City*. The music for *The Pursued* was traditional, and *Scherzo* and *The Unsleeping City* both were musically scored by Florence Greenberg. Early that summer, Mary and Joe gave their first independent concert at Wheaton College in Massachusetts. Later in 1948, Mary and Joe performed together at various colleges and in Colorado.

In the late 1940s, Mary did her first master solo concert and taught master classes at Louisiana State University. During the solo performance, the weather was exceptionally hot and humid, and Mary struggled to change her costumes. They literally had to be peeled off her body. And, because it was a solo concert, time was of the essence between her solos. This is one of the many challenges of touring. A few times Mary was slow and a bit late to return to the stage, but the audience thought she was worth the wait.

In July 1948, Mary was having lunch with a visiting friend from the Midwest. As they were walking down the street, they ran into Bill Bales who said, "Mary, you're just the person I want to see. A whole new repertory company is starting up that is going to have dance and stage productions, and I want you to be a part of it." Mary's friend from the Midwest thought this was how Broadway casting worked: Someone might say, "Would you like to be in a Broadway show?" and you would respond "Well, if I'm not too busy." Mary explained that it doesn't really work like that until you become established. Eventually, Mary did become involved with this new repertory company. The people with whom Mary worked were Uta Hagen and Herbert Berghof, along with Bill Bales as the choreographer. Among the four of them, they had a great many talents. Logically, this combination would have created work for two years and might even turn into something like the Stanislavsky Theater in Russia (Konstantin Stanislavsky is famous for his acting system that he created). Unfortunately, they chose to do *Rip Van Winkle* for their first program. It ran two weeks and closed. Mary had a speaking part as well as dance, and she adored the combination of dancing and acting. And, Bill Bales really created good choreography. Despite this disappointment, Mary continued working with Uta and Herbert teaching actors to dance in their acting studio.

The *Rip Van Winkle* flop created acute disappointment in Mary, and she had not been in touch with Hanya during this period. At this time, Hanya was holding auditions for her next musical, *Kiss Me Kate*. Although Mary needed the work that Hanya could provide, she didn't call Hanya to ask any favors for *Kiss Me Kate*. Mary knew Hanya wanted dancers to earn their own way, Mary went to the audition along with everyone else. A few days later, she ran into a dancer from the audition on the street, who asked her if she had received by mail the notice of the final call-back audition. Unfortunately, Mary had not, so she assumed that for some reason, Hanya didn't want her in this show. Therefore, Mary didn't want to simply show up to the call-back audition, because that would put Hanya on the spot. Mary figured she had worked with Hanya for several years, and Hanya should know her work by this time. As it turns out, Hanya had sent Mary the final notice, but she never received it in the mail. Hanya waited for 15 minutes to start the audition, waiting for Mary. When Mary didn't arrive, Hanya moved ahead with the audition and selected her cast. *Kiss Me Kate* was an outstanding show, and Mary would have liked to be a part of it.

Richard Price

Mary Anthony and Joseph Gifford in "The Pursued", choreographed by Joseph Gifford, photo by Mary Cook Marett

Mary Anthony and Joseph Gifford in "The Unsleeping City", choreographed by Joseph Gifford

Mary Anthony and Joseph Gifford in "Chaconne", choreographed by Mary Anthony, photo by William Korff

Mary Anthony in her choreography of "Chaconne"

Mary Anthony in her choreography of "Chaconne"

A Dancer's Journey "It All Started With A Lie" 45

Mary Anthony in her choreography of "Lady Macbeth", photo by Kenn Duncan

Mary Anthony in her choreography of "Lady Macbeth", photo by Mary Cook Marett

Mary Anthony and Joseph Gifford in "Scherzo", choreographed by Joseph Gifford

Mary Anthony in front of the "Rip Van Winkle" marquee in 1947

Mary Anthony, 1949, photo by Louis Renault

CHAPTER 4

"Touch and Go," The Musical

Following her disappointments with *Rip Van Winkle* and the *Kiss Me Kate* auditions, Mary heard about a new Broadway musical *Touch and Go*, a revue of humorous sketches, to be choreographed by Helen Tamiris. Mary had always admired Helen's work, as Helen created strong personal statements through modern dance. In addition to rebelling against poverty, racism, greed, and war, Helen also made her mark choreographing to Negro spirituals. Helen had a wide repertoire of choreography. As Helen performed less herself, she started choreographing musicals.

Because Helen was chorgeographing *Touch and Go*, she wanted to audition, but there was one big problem. The audition was set for the day Mary was scheduled to leave for Colorado to perform and teach with Joe Gifford. The day before the audition, Mary figured that Helen was probably at the theater, so she walked down to try to arrange an alternate audition time. Unfortunately, it was pouring rain. By the time Mary arrived at the theater, she was dripping wet in her skirt and blouse. A men's audition was in progress. Realizing she should have brought her dance clothes, she turned to leave, but Helen saw her and asked her to stay. Once the men had finished, Helen introduced Mary to George Abbott (playwright, producer, director, and screenwriter), and she asked Mary to perform something for him. Mary took off her shoes, and in her dripping wet clothes, she improvised for approximately five minutes. When finished, she explained her schedule conflict and really didn't think she had any chance of being cast in the show.

While in Colorado, Mary and Joe taught and performed at the University of Colorado. Cameron McCosh had been hired from Denver as the pianist for Mary's modern dance classes. As Mary and Cameron worked together, they became very good friends. This was the beginning of a powerful relationship in both of their lives. Also during this trip, Mary received a telegram asking her to report to rehearsal for *Touch and Go* in New York soon after her engagement ended. Helen had cast her in the show after all! Before Mary left Colorado, Fran Doughtery, a teacher at the University of Colorado, and Cameron McCosh convinced Mary that she needed to see the Rocky Mountains. As fate would have it, on this very excursion, they became snowbound up in the mountains. And this was in August! Mary was unable to get back to New York for her first Broadway rehearsal. She sent a telegram to New York saying she was snowbound and would be 48 hours late. She wasn't even sure if they would believe her, as it was hot and steamy in New York. As upset as she was at the time, the irony of the situation became a good joke later on.

Mary loved George Abbott. He loved dancers, and he loved to dance. Other dancers in *Touch and Go* were Daniel Nagrin (lead), Pearl Lang (one of the leads), and five male dancers: David Lober, Bobby Griffith, John Fealy, Xavier Francis, and Jonathan Lucas. They started dance rehearsals several weeks before the official show rehearsals. They began working on a ballet focused on the cartoon character Dick Tracy. Helen allowed Mary to choreograph some of her own sections by giving her direction with a story line. This ballet consumed most of the dancers' rehearsals, but when they opened in New Haven, Connecticut, the producers were not enthusiastic. They did let Helen keep changing and working on the choreography, but in the end it had to be cut. The producers accepted all the other numbers. The musical *Touch and Go* had sketches and lyrics by Jean and Walter Kerr and music by Jay Gorney. On October 14, 1949 the New York *Times*' writer Brooks Atkinson wrote,

> Serving as his own director, Mr. Kerr (Walter) has populated his cartoon with an especially winning cast of young professionals who can dance, sing and act out a joke without feeling smug about it.

Without the Dick Tracy ballet, the dancers quickly needed something to take its place for their opening in Philadelphia. The composer and the lyricist liked Pearl, Mary, David, and Danny in particular; in fact, they wrote a ballet for the four dancers called *Under the Sleeping Volcano*, a dramatic story that took place in Mexico. When the dancers arrived in Philadelphia, they worked one full day with Helen, and by 8 PM they were finished with the new ballet. Helen was so focused on getting the choreography done, that she had forgotten that all the other dancers in the show had also been called for that same rehearsal. These dancers had been sitting around all day, while Helen worked with just the four select dancers. When she realized this situation, she called other dancers up onto the stage to rehearse a jazz number. Pearl was tired, and she excused herself from the extended rehearsal. But Mary stayed to help. Helen wanted the dancers to do a very complicated jump, which they were unable to do. Asking Mary to demonstrate the jump many times, Helen was sure the dancers would be able to pick it up. Still, the dancers were unable to do the jump, and after several more demonstrations by a very tired Mary, they heard a horrendous sound—like two boards being clapped together. In a daze, Mary heard herself screaming in pain. When Mary came to, she was lying on the floor and had a mound of ice on her left foot, and Daniel Nagrin was attempting to pour brandy down her throat. George Abbott, Helen, and Daniel put Mary into a cab and headed to the emergency room. The doctor on call was in a tuxedo; they realized he had obviously come from a formal event. Before he could even do an X-ray, they were asking him if Mary's foot was fractured. The X-ray didn't show a break, so the doctor declared it a bad sprain. For several days, Mary hobbled around teaching all of her parts, and as she did, her foot grew bigger and bigger. A follow-up x-ray revealed that Mary's foot was indeed broken in two places. By hobbling around on her sprained foot, she ended up breaking it. Dancers never know when to stop!

George, thankfully, loved Mary's dancing and her work ethic. He kept her on full salary the entire time of her recuperation, paying all her medical expenses as well. He told Mary that when she was able to get back on her feet, he wanted her back in the show.

Mary continued teaching her parts, and as she did, she discovered that when she taught without being able to demonstrate, it made her a better teacher. Instead, she had to verbally tell everyone what to do. After her foot had nearly healed, she returned to most of her original parts in the show, but not in the number *Under the Sleeping Volcano*, as it was too strenuous for a healing foot. Ultimately, *Touch and Go* was a very successful musical show on Broadway, and in 1950, Helen Tamiris won the Tony Award as the show's choreographer.

One day when Mary arrived at the theater, George asked her if she would like to go to London. Mary said, "Of course," but she thought he was joking. Bobby Griffith, stage manager, and Hal Prince, producer, and his assistant came into Mary's dressing room. During their conversation, they told Mary that George was very serious about going to London. In fact, that very night, an English producer was in the audience and came backstage to meet Mary after the show. He wanted *Touch and Go* in London. Because Helen couldn't leave the New York show, she recommended Mary to take her place. After the show that night, the English producer asked Mary if she could choreograph several new ballets for the London version, because some of the numbers were too "Americana" for London. With Helen's and Abbott's blessing, Mary accepted this exciting opportunity.

When Mary left the Broadway *Touch and Go*, Ilona Murai took all of Mary's parts; Mary thought she was a very good replacement.

Before Mary left for London, she asked Helen for advice on how to handle an audition and what to expect as choreographer. Helen explained that she would have no friends who were in the show. Also, she continued, if you have tall boys, hire tall girls. And, if you have short boys, hire short girls.

When Mary went to London, she brought with her Helen Gallager, who had been in the New York show, along with Kay Ballard, David Lober, and five additional dancers. One of the five was Jonathan Lucas, who eventually became a very good television choreographer. *Touch and Go* opened at the Prince of Wales Theatre in London in April 1950.

During this time, Mary was still teaching at the New Dance Group. Her professional class was excited for her opportunity in London; at the same time, however, they were sad to see her leave New York. This class consisted of Doris Hering, John Fealy, Xavier Francis, and Ronnie Aul. All of these dancers met Mary at the ship as it pulled away from the dock in New York. Mary loved this particular class, as they took her technique class six days a week, followed by a workshop class of improvised individual compositions. She found it very difficult to leave these dancers behind.

The ship to England was called the Queen Mary. Not long after leaving New York, it encountered a hurricane. (This was likely Hurricane Two, which formed on August 23, 1949 and traveled up the eastern coast of the United States.) While all of the other passengers were seasick in their rooms, the dancers were totally unaffected by the ship rocking back and forth amidst the tempest. In fact, they were in absolute heaven, having full run of the ship. The dancers indulged in all three meals each day and danced throughout the ship. As they danced, the ship's orchestra played. Dancers do have incredible balance even in stormy waters! When the storm subsided, the passengers emerged, coming up to the dining room and other spaces. The dancers' fun was over.[12]

When Mary arrived in London, she didn't have enough modern dancers, so she was able to perform all of her old parts, including *Under the Sleeping Volcano*. For the trip to London, Mary's friend Helen Gallagher had a marvelous agent, who managed all the arrangements for all of the salaries of the American performers. The Americans had to actually spend their entire income in England, as they were not allowed to take any English money out of the country. To help them use part of their income, Mary, Helen Gallaher, and Kay Ballard rented a three-story house on the Thames River that was three doors away from T. S. Elliot's place. Kay occupied the first floor, and Mary and Helen had the second story. Together, they all enjoyed the third-floor balcony that overlooked the Thames. They would eat their breakfast there and laugh, talk, and enjoy the view. This was a very happy time for all of them.

When they first landed on British shores, they purchased bikes so they could explore the countryside. This was before they realized how much energy the shows required. Mary wasn't really able to use her bike until later in France. Since Mary was in Europe, she extended her stay so that she would be able to visit France.

Because the dancers had to use their money in England, they took taxi cabs everywhere. This was shortly after World War II, when rationing was still in place, and English people were only able to get a pound of coffee per month, one egg per week per person, no meat, and no heat. With the theaters so cold, the dancers wore their coats backstage, only taking them off when they went onstage. And, as Americans who had not personally experienced bombing as most of Europe had, living in postwar London gave the dancers a new appreciation for the reality and devastation of war. There were still places in London where one could see the effects of the exploding German rockets. Their landlady told them stories about constantly going into hiding during the air raids. At a certain point, she quit going into hiding and left her life in the hands of fate.

David Lober, another dancer in the show, came from the Lester Horton dance background, the same background as Alvin Ailey, James Truitte, Carmen de Lavellade, and Joyce Trisler. David was very supportive of Mary and her work. He helped her with the choreography of the jazz number in the show, as Mary wasn't as familiar with jazz as he was. The two of them discovered that they had a lot in common. Many times, they would talk all night about poetry, music, and the astrology. They are both Scorpios.

Mary, Helen, and David undertook all kinds of fun activities together. Helen Gallagher was pure innocence and very naïve. Although they were cold from the lack of heat, they all look back to this English time with wonderful, warm London memories. It is funny how dancers can spend a year together working and playing, but when the show finishes, they hardly ever see each other. Mary and Helen were a perfect example of this. Mary thought it was strange to work so closely with someone, and after that to see them very little or not at all.

Touch and Go ran a full year in London. During the run, Mary, David, and Helen received an unsigned note backstage that said, "Could you please meet us at the corner of Lester Square Road and another crossroad on Sunday morning at 10 AM?" It ended up that Mary was the only one of the three who went to the appointed meeting, as the other two didn't take it seriously. There Mary was met by Ermino Macario, a famous Italian comedian, and three other gentlemen who were connected with show business in Italy. They had seen *Touch and Go* and wanted to produce a modern dance musical in Italy. They wanted Mary to choreograph an Italian musical for them. With this invitation, Mary asked for a leave of absence from the show in London in order to go to Italy, which the management allowed her. Mary also asked if she could take David and Helen, but they drew the line; Mary was the only one permitted to go.

The name of the Italian musical was *Votate Per Venere* which means Vote for Venus. According to the plot, if you vote for the goddess of love this act would save the world. The Italian musicals were built around

Ermino Marcario, who performed in the style of Charlie Chaplin and Buster Keaton. The comedians did the sketches, in which they did not say a word, and then there would be five to seven minutes of pure movement with an idea behind it. *Votate Per Venere* took place in September 1950.

Mary was changed for life with this Italian experience. During this time, Mary lived in Rome on the Via Sistina. She loved the richness of the sunlight, the warmth of the people, and especially the Italian menu. She discovered that the food and the Italian eating schedule fit her life perfectly. Italians had breakfast in the morning and ate their largest meal in the middle of the day, which was followed by a two-hour nap. Following their nap, they would have a coffee and rehearse until 10 PM. At the very end of the day, they finished with a small meal.

Cameron McCosh was the pianist and dancer that Mary had met in Colorado when she was there with Joseph Gifford. While Mary was in Europe, he came to meet her there. With the money she made in Italy, the two vacationed in Paris where they rented a little flat from a French landlady called "Madame," who loved artists. She hated charging them the $11 rent, so she was always giving them gifts such as Turkish bells and fruits and vegetables from her garden. The apartment was small but the perfect size for the two of them. They spent much of their time out in the beautiful garden for which the Madame so meticulously cared. Shops for bread, meats, and cheese were within walking distance. Mary and Cameron rode their bicycles for more than 1,000 miles using their apartment as their home base. On some of their bicycle trips, they camped out and one time, Mary remembers even sleeping on a merry-go-round. They also stayed in hostels in Europe, where all of the people would sit around and share stories and food. Mary and Cameron also bicycled throughout Switzerland.

One of their excursions took them through the Pyrenees into Spain. But when they arrived at the border of Spain, the custom's guard asked for their visa to enter the country. As they didn't have a visa to enter Spain, he told them they could not enter. They convinced the guard to just let them step over the border so they could put their toes into the lake that was right by the border. Now, they would be able to say they had been to Spain.

While Mary and Cameron lived together in France, she got pregnant. Both she and Cameron were excited with the thought of having a child. But one night, Mary was awakened by fumes coming from the coal burning stove, which were making her sick. In the dark, she groped her way to the bathroom, knocking over a huge bookcase that fell on her. Unfortunately, this caused Mary to miscarry. For a long while, Mary felt it was just fate. But in hindsight, she would have loved to have had Cameron's child. While in Paris she could not have known that their future together would be cut short and another opportunity would not present itself. He was the love of her life.

Sailing back from Europe, Mary and Cameron were on the ship *S. S. De Grasse*. They performed on the ship just because they wanted to. The captain, delighted with this arrangement, gave them nicer living quarters in exchange for performing. Mary and Cameron had originally arrived in New York toward the beginning of 1952, and on their return from Europe, Cameron played for dance classes at The New Dance Group while Mary taught. Mary and Cameron delighted in working together. He would listen to Mary's choreographic ideas and compose music for her. Mary choreographed *The Devil in Massachusetts* to Cameron's composition, and it premiered on March 6, 1952 at the 92nd Street YMHA in New York City.

The producers in Italy wanted Mary to stay, and although she loved Italy, the sun, the lifestyle, and the work, she would always return to New York. In Mary's words, "There is an energy in New York City that is nowhere else on earth." She returned to Italy every fall and choreographed musicals and television for them each year through 1954. In the fall of 1952, Mary choreographed *Billiardo*, and in 1953 she choreographed *Barbanera...bel tempo si Spera* staring Ugo Tognazzi and Elena Giusti. Ronne Aul was in this work, and he ended up staying in Italy.

On her returns to New York each year, Mary danced with the City Center Opera Ballet (later called New York City Opera Ballet). Although "ballet" was in the title of the company, it really consisted of modern dance. Some of the modern dancers were Mary, Mary Hinkson, Glen Tetley, Al Shuman, and Don Redlich. At this time, the main choreographer was John Butler.

Her first performance with the opera ballet was *Bluebeard's Castle* in 1952, which still holds special memories for Mary. John Butler did the staging and choreography to the Bartok opera, and Lincoln Kirsten produced the show. The Opera spent a significant amount of money on this production. Mary's costume alone, which was encrusted with jewels and sequins, was $1,000, and her wig was $350. Never before had the opera spent money on costumes such as this. Before this show opened, dancers wore the same skirts with different tops for various operas. Now, with this opera's new funding, they had new costumes for the performers. Walter Terry, critic for the New York *Herald Tribune*,[13] was so excited with John Butler's choreography and staging, he called it, "...a new peak of power for the art dance in the lyric theater." In the New York *Times* on October 3, 1952, critic Olin Downes wrote a description of the plot in his review.[14] Downes wrote,

> The New York City Opera offered a double bill last night in the City Center of Music and Drama, consisting of the first stage performance in America of Bela Bartok's opera, *Bluebeard's Castle*....There are two characters who converse and philosophize eternally. Judith wants to know all the secrets, all the facets, of her husband's soul. She will unlock not only the seventh door, but every one of them, to reveal his

secret and free him of it. She wants to know too much. She therefore is relegated to the ranks of Bluebeard's former wives, each one of whom he adores for what she meant to him, but to no one of whom will he reveal his entire nature or creative purpose.

Mary Anthony was the third door, Mary Hinkson was Judith's inner self, Anneliese Widman with Alvin Shulman was the fourth door, and Glen Tetley was the sixth door.

Because many operas are quite long, Mary came to the theater to perform the first act, left the theater to teach, and returned to the theater to dance in the fourth act. Mary delighted in doing two things at the same time!

In 1953, Mary performed at the Ziegfeld Theatre at the end of February and early March. She danced in Charles Weidman's *Fables For Our Time* with Charles Weidman, Carl Morris, and Betty Osgood. *Fables For Our Time* is a work that features four comic fables from James Thurber that are set to music by Freda Miller. *Fables for Our Time* featured a disgruntled husband, a chipmunk who preferred to play with acorns rather than collecting them, a foolish owl, and a lazy beaver. Dance critic Walter Terry wrote, "Charles Weidman once more provided the audience with unmatched examples of danced pantomime, humor, penetrating, impudent and wonderfully human."[15]

Years before, Mary had seen a performance of Katrina Paxton Greek Company in New York City. The company performed *Electra*, and the members of the company both acted and danced. For Mary, it was "total theater"—performance that incorporated dance, acting, and all aspects of theater. The performance made her think deeply about the desire to be a dancer versus an actress. Thus, her goals began to be take shape—her dancers would be actors. Seeing this company perform also confirmed her ideas about how she wanted to train her students. Mary says, "The face is the most important muscle you have." Giving vivid imagery so that each step speaks volumes, Mary trains the entire dancer. The Katrina Paxton Greek Company also planted the seed of the name that she would give to her own dance company when she was ready: Mary Anthony Dance Theatre.

For Mary, many events happened in 1954. Between trips to Italy to choreograph *Barbanera*, she opened her own studio; performed, choreographed, and staged works at the White Barn Theater; and performed in Hadassah's East Indian concert. For Hadassah, she performed as the evil signs of Shiva. Remy Charlip made her mask with a cake cooling rack. After the performance, Mary's face was imprinted with red stripes where the cake rack had been. Steve Vendola, who later danced with Alwin Nikolais, performed with Mary in this piece.

With the opening of her studio behind her, Mary could really settle down with her own school and develop her dancers in her evolving choreography and technique. This was a new chapter in Mary's life.

Mary Anthony in Italy

Mary Anthony in Italy

Mary Anthony teaching in Italy

Mary Anthony and Cameron McCosh at Jones Beach

Mary Anthony at Jones Beach

Mary Anthony at Jones Beach

left to right - Esta Beck, Cameron McCosh, and Mary Anthony at Jones Beach

Mary Anthony at Jones Beach

Mary Anthony directing and teaching in Italy

Choreographer Mary Anthony with the Director of "Barbanera" in Italy

"Fables for Our Time" choreographed by Charles Weidman

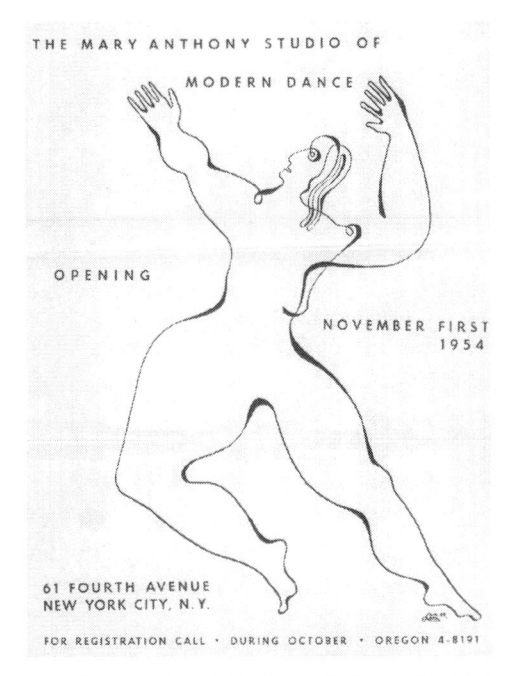

Poster from the opening of the Mary Anthony Studio in 1954, art work by Alfred Van Loen

Mary Anthony, summer 1954 on Mantauk

CHAPTER 5

"*Think of Your Buttocks as Apples and Prick them with Toothpicks*"– *The Birth of Mary Anthony's School and the Mary Anthony Dance Theatre*

Mary wanted her own studio for many reasons. After teaching the Hanya Holm technique at Hanya's school and later at the New Dance Group, she wanted to branch out on her own, explore her own way of moving, and develop her own principles. Board meetings at the New Dance Group were pointlessly time consuming, in that everyone had his or her own point of view, and they had difficulty coming to a consensus. Mary was ready to live by her own point of view and the studio gave her the freedom to do just that. Grateful for the variety of dance styles she had learned at the New Dance Group, she felt inspired to discover her own approach. Plus, the classes she had taught at the New Dance Group were not only packed, but had a waiting list. Feeling confident her students would follow her, she opened her own studio.

First, Mary needed a space, ideally a loft space. Fortunately, her good friend Alfred Van Loen had a huge loft at 61 Fourth Avenue that he was willing to trade for her small apartment on Greenwich Avenue. Alfred was an artist who created sculptures and didn't need much space—in fact, he preferred do his work in a smaller environment. So they swapped, and together, they knocked down walls and put up beams in Mary's new studio. They made a dressing room and created a tiny place in the back for Mary to live—very "Japanese-style" as was Mary's desire to keep it small and simple. Later, Alfred moved to Huntington, Long Island, where he worked in a studio of an old farm house. True to his European roots, he loved the wide open country house surrounded with apple trees.

The money Mary made from her 1954 fall Italian musical was money that enabled her to open her own dance studio in New York City. After she had set everything up for her new studio, she returned later from Italy than she had hoped. Mary's close friend and Holm dancer Annaleise Widman was present in her place for the grand opening of the Mary Anthony Dance Studio in December 1954 at 61 Fourth Avenue.

To Mary's surprise, only six students followed her. Discouraged, she went to Alfred for advice. Both he and photographer Alan Haas gave Mary the same advice: businesses start small; each day it would grow bigger, and she must persevere. Fortunately, Mary was still dancing for the City Center Opera Ballet, which made it financially possible to grow her studio.

Mary had received a great education with Hanya Holm, including techniques to use Laban's movement in space. Rudolf Laban is known in particular for his notation of dance, which includes his famous arm swings. In his own book *A Life for Dance*, he writes, "In dancing we are able to express relationships in which awareness of self and others is enhanced. The feeling of joy which dance can give helps us to harmonize ourselves and gain an increased sense of belonging." According to Mary, Hanya's greatest contribution to dance was creating teachers, and Martha Graham's contribution was producing performers. Mary wanted to bridge the gap between these two greats. She wanted to create a technique for all dancers regardless of physical limitations. She found Martha Graham's technique difficult for dancers with tight knees and tight pelvises, and she wanted to cater to those dancers. Mary was ready to explore the truth in floor work and movement exercises. Mary said,[16]

> I feel that floor work is important. First of all, it takes away the problem of balance while you are getting the spine and the abdominal muscles strong enough to perform certain things. But it has much deeper meaning to me, and I use this when I work with actors. [In floor work you are close to the earth, and there is an earth energy that you may not be conscious of but that is coming to you through this act of working on the floor.]

In many modern techniques such as Mary's, the dancer is part of the earth and uses the gravity of the earth in movement, unlike ballet in which the dancer is moving away from the earth to become more ethereal. Mary went on to say,

> I think it [floor work] is one of the things modern dance contributed, because in ballet at this time, to be on the floor was to die. It never occurred to ballet choreographers that you could go to the floor as a method of being reborn and springing back up to new life. So for me, the floor work had those two elements: first of all, a kind of centering where you did not have to depend on balance for that centering. And [secondly] there is an energy that comes from the floor.

Mary also believes that the teacher is not only teaching technique but also teaching the dancer how to grow as a performer. She said,

I happen to be one of those old fashioned people who believe that the performance starts in the classroom. That is where you begin to make it happen, day after day after day. And then you carry it further in rehearsal. I think there is a great art to constructive rehearsing, where you grow at each rehearsal instead of repeating at each rehearsal. So when that dreadful night comes, and you have been on a bus, and you arrive at the theater, and you are going to perform that very night at 8 PM, you are so trained to perform that you give a performance that night.

Mary even went beyond this in developing the dancer as a human being. When the dancer enters the Mary Anthony studio, her mission statement is displayed prominently: "The intention of this school will be to inspire the student to the realization of self; physically through the discipline of dance training; emotionally through formal creativity."

Once Mary had her own studio, she was free to develop her own classroom approach. For example, she added an assortment of torso and arm movements to the basic warm-up exercises. Mary said,

> Through center standing work, you really do what I call the Czerny of music exercises in dance. You have the plié, and you have the brush, and they have to be done every day, including Saturday and Sunday…I add all kinds of challenges on top of those plié … where I would do different arms, or add a head or something.

An article by Josephine Fox came out in *Dance Magazine* 11 years after the opening of her studio, which was in 1954 in March 1965 titled, "The Day is Mine, the Land is Mine." It discussed Mary's teaching in her studio. Fox wrote,

> 'Think of your buttocks as apples and prick them with toothpicks,' Mary admonishes her class. 'Now let me see you move across the floor.' Minutes later she describes a church that she saw in France, and then introduces a combination that resulted from visual experience. Or, it is reference to the Greeks—a civilization she invariably refers to with special flourish. Noting the limp, lifeless arms and shoulders of a dancer, she frowns and then in a good-natured scolding voice exhorts, 'You are wearing weights of golden bracelets from Crete—don't have puppet's arms…' What a curious way to instruct dancers, when it is the body that must be disciplined. But for Mary Anthony, it is not enough to guide with a brusque 'tighten the buttocks, lift the arms.' The imagination must first be nourished, she believes, then the body comes alive.

Noting Mary's use of images, Fox wrote, "She is forever enveloping the dancer in an atmosphere of imagery...about the spine, she will tell you it is a tumbleweed, a whiplash, a shining inner light. When you dance, you are a lovely black panther moving through a golden jungle."

Mary felt this imagery would help a dancer transform from a technical dancer to a performing artist. Using further imagery, Mary said,[17]

> Going through space, where space is like an active thing, that can either be like a tail wind for an airplane, where it speeds you up, or it can be an active thing that you have to go through, and struggle through, and I feel that this whirling through space is the preparing the dancer for the act of performing, because when you finally ultimately perform in the theater, you are usually whirling through space.

Constantly drawing from her excursions to art museums, Mary would incorporate specific images into her technique. For example, in the painting *The Scream* by Edvard Munch, she would ask the dancers to feel the anguish of the painting. Fox made the same observation in her article when she wrote, "The divining rod in Miss Anthony's teaching is her ability to seek out and capture moments—moments of bliss, anguish, discovery of another person, of oneself. By doing this, she approaches dance as though it was acting."

One of Mary's classes was a workshop class that taught dancers to act and actors to move. Deep basic Stanislavski acting principles were imbedded in her work, which she had learned as a theater major in college.

When Mary teaches her dancers how to choreograph, she uses a different method than Anna Sokolow, famous choreographer who taught at her studio and whose works are in the repertory of major dance companies worldwide. Anna follows the concepts of Louis Horst in that the choreography comes from a musical base, in which you have to know a theme, a structure, and form. Because this is innately a part of Mary's being, she naturally incorporates this philosophy into her technique classes. In Mary's workshop classes, however, she goes beyond this and leads the dancers to explore dramatic concepts and improvisational directions and challenges. Over and over, Mary has stated that you must be totally aware of what you are doing. If you do something wonderful, you could do it 100 times. You don't just fling yourself around. Mary gives the dancers and actors a concept and stresses over and over that the more you limit improvisation (in implementing a concept), the greater the result will be. For example, when Mary teaches students concepts in the Stanislavski method, she has been known to say to them, "If you know [1] who you are, [2] where you are, [3] when in time is it? A long time ago? Yesterday? The future? [4] what are you doing? and [5] why are you doing it? With that in mind, if you can answer these five questions clearly, the dance is already half done."

Mary's first piece of choreography after opening the school was *Women of Troy*. It was first performed in 1954 at the New Dance Group Festival in New York City with Donald McKayle and Arthur Mitchell, who both went on to become award-winning and legendary figures in American dance. Years later, when Mary was trying to restage the work, Mary and Donald were trying to recall the original choreography, but they were having a very difficult time. Worse yet, Mary no longer had the original music. Cameron McCosh was the original composer and musician when it was performed. For her rehearsals, he had given Mary a long-playing record (an "LP") with only the underlying beat. Unfortunately, by that time he had passed away, leaving her with only a recording of the essential melody line. Mary asked Elliot Weiss, a long-time friend, music associate, and dance accompanist if he could compose the score by just hearing the underlying beat and knowing the story of her choreographic work. Indeed, he could, and the score emerged beautifully. During this same period, Mary choreographed *Trio*, and its first performance included Mary, Anneliese Widman, and Harvey Lichtenstein.

From 1955–1957, Mary continued performing with John Butler Dance Theater at Brooklyn Academy of Music, and she performed in the choreography of John Butler and Charles Weidman at the City Center Opera Ballet in New York City. Some of the operas in which Mary danced were *Bluebeard's Castle*, *Traviata*, *Don Giavoni*, *Carmen*, and *Aida*.

Mary had a long-time friend, Marvin Silbersher, who worked for CBS. He was a great actor, playwright, and Renaissance man. In 1956, he came to Mary's studio to ask her if she would be interested in choreographing *The Lord's Prayer*. Thinking he was joking, she said "Sure, just give me a call." That same night, Marvin called Mary and told her he wasn't joking, as he had been appointed the new director of an existing Sunday morning program called *Look Up and Live*. To this point, the show had been merely a sermon by a minister, but the television network was revamping the program to meet the audience—mostly teenagers—who stayed home on Sunday mornings. This new format would include dramatic concepts: jazz, dance, movement, poetry, and various creative ways to appeal, they hoped, to the teenagers who were not attending church. The program *Look Up and Live* was supported by Protestants, Jews, and Catholics. Mary would have to audition her choreography in front of a panel of representatives from each religion, and after obtaining their approval, she would be given free reign. Her choreography of the *The Lord's Prayer* was her audition. To prepare, Mary, Cameron, and Annaliese went to the Metropolitan Museum of Art to study the paintings of Fra Angelico, an early Renaissance painter who painted religious subjects. Finding his art inspirational, Mary began to choreograph.

Mary vividly remembers her evaluation. The panel entered the studio with stone faces. In front of this pessimistic group, Mary's group performed *The Lord's Prayer*, and it was very successful. In fact, one of the nuns, with tears in her eyes, approached Mary and said, "I never dreamed it could be done, I never did."

In April 1956, Doris Hering reviewed Mary's ninth program in *Dance Magazine*. The performance was broadcast on February 26, 1956 and featured the story of Elijah and Jezebel.[18]

Hering wrote,

> It all began at 10:30 in the morning when the Mary Anthony Dance Theatre illumined the story of Elijah on CBS-TV's *Look Up and Live*. This modestly-budget-program, which is produced with the cooperation of the National Council of Churches of Christ in America, frequently uses dance as the handmaiden of religion—which make it something of a phenomenon. The dancing is usually mimetic, with a spoken narration in the background and a verbal summation by the Reverend Charles Templeton...
>
> This particular program, the ninth that Mary Anthony has done for the series, followed the prophet Elijah (Joseph Gifford) in his search for the 'still small voice' of truth. The major flaw in the program's approach was a surfeit of words. Director Marv Silbersher relied upon a danced continuity, but he did not have the courage to let the dance make its points without verbal intrusion and explanation.

In October 1956 an article called "Modern Dancers Find Mime a Talent Beneath the Skin" appeared in... The author stated,[19]

> ...the Mary Anthony Dance Group has been utilizing unspoken dramatic idea vignettes to point up some Christian ethic. The philosophy behind the mime playlet is then summed up by a minister at the conclusion of the half-hour, with occasional comment interspersed with the action. On October 23, Sunday, at 10:30 AM over CBS channel 2, *Look Up and Live* presented the problem of Sam Jones, Suburban Everyman, confused, lacking a soul, a victim of scrambled ethics and addicted to the white lie to save him from embarrassing situations. Sam invents appointments to avoid people he does not want to see, carps about speeders but breaks traffic rules himself, tries to cheat on his railway ticket, etc., then tries to lecture his children on honesty and the 'golden rule.' When his boss, a malevolent dictator, orders him to fire an old trusted woman employee in favor of a younger, prettier edition of the sex, Sam finally rebels, and for the first time in his life takes a stand according to his inner-most conscience. Fired for failing to knuckle under, he goes home in fear, but finds his family four-square behind him. Somewhat reborn, he faces the future unafraid. The entire

presentation was achieved in pantomime, along with some comments from a narrator and reverend. Dancers include Mary Anthony, choreographer, Joseph Gifford, Anneliese Widman, Irving Burton, Emily Thompson, and Dick Colcino.

In the fall of 1956, Mary was invited to teach and choreograph at Bennington, replacing Bill Bales who was on a sabbatical. While at Bennington, Mary lived in a little farmhouse named "Cricket Hill." Every morning, she had the studio to herself with no telephones ringing, no office work, no studio problems, nothing to distract her. She had three days each week in solitude as she continued to run her studio, commuting back and forth from New York City. This proved to be a very creative time for Mary, as she was not only choreographing for *Look Up and Live* and creating a work for the Bennington dancers, but also planting the seeds of new choreography for her upcoming company premiere in mid-December.

Many of the students that Mary worked with at Bennington were seniors who eventually joined her company. When she arrived at the college, she gave the dancers a proposal of four possible pieces of choreography. To Mary's delight the dancers chose what would become *Threnody*.

Two years before, Mary had the idea to choreograph the story *Riders to the Sea*, a play written by John Millington Synge, which she called *Threnody*. Originally, she wanted Anneliese Widman to dance in this new work, because she was also a marvelous actress and dancer. Anneliese was married to a playwright, who told Mary she was out of her mind to choreograph this famous story. He said it was a perfect one-act play, and he felt no one should touch it, much less choreograph it. It did give Mary pause, as she respected him, but she continued to contemplate the possibilities. Unfortunately, Anneliese was involved in various projects when Mary wanted to work with her. She also wanted Laura Sheleen to be in this work. Before she got the opportunity to choreograph it, however, Laura had moved to Paris. Mary thought of the many students she had taught from the New Dance Group, but they had not followed her when she opened her studio. With the loss of Annaliese, Lara, and her many students, Mary grieved deeply. In this way, however, she could relate to the mother in *Riders to the Sea*.

Mary found the music for *Threnody* quite by accident. Mary already had a record of Benjamin Britten's *Diversion of the Left Hand*—a piece she had done for television. One day, she just happened to listen to the other side of this record and discovered *Sinfonia de Requiem* would be the perfect music for *Threnody*.

The story for *Threnody* starts with the action of a mother cradling a rope that represents all the sons she has lost to the sea, as well as the remaining one she hopes to save from the same tragedy. After the mother's exit, her two daughters examine a package that has washed ashore, and they discover that it contains a shirt of a brother lost at sea. The mother returns to tell the daughters of a vision (which the audience sees), in which her dead older son returns to take her younger son to the sea. The mother then experiences a flashback to a time when all her sons were alive, fishing and dancing with their sweethearts. But her flashback returns to the vivid reality that her sons are lost forever. The last part of the dance is the formal lament (the threnody) for all who live and die by the sea.

December 6, 1956 was the premiere performance of *Threnody* at Bennington College set on the Bennington dancers. Mary proved the cynics wrong—the work was a success. A few days later, December 13, Mary Anthony Dance Theatre was born, with its first New York performance at the YM and YWHA (Young Men's and Young Women's Hebrew Association) located at Lexington Avenue and 92nd Street to a sold out audience. The repertory for her first company performance was *Aperitif, Portraits* (in two parts: Part 1 was *Chaconne* with music by Wolpe, and Part 2 was *Giga* with music by Bach); *Trio* with music by Brahms; *Threnody* with music by Britten; and *Songs* with music by Debussy. Its three parts (*Little Lamb Who Made Thee, Tyger, Tyger Burning Bright,* and *Each Shall Seek His Own*) were modeled after William Blake's *Songs of Innocence and of Experience* and Sidney Morse's *Centennial Hymn*. *Songs* was choreographed from Mary's experience of being young and in love with Cameron McCosh. It featured three young couples in love and a mother figure. For this first concert, Tom Skelton was the production manager.

This first company of dancers were Alice Uchida, Joy Gitlin, Joseph Cino, Angelo Lo Vullo, Louis McKenzie, Diane Diener, Shaque Holobigian, Dick Cuyler, Cameron McCosh, Don Price, and guests Anneliese Widman and the Bennington College Dance Group who performed in *Threnody*. These first company members were special to Mary, even after they left the company, and she kept up with how their lives progressed. For example, years later Joy Gitlin got married and had two sons. One day she returned to Mary's studio to take class. Joy told Mary, "Well, we used to go lots of places for technique, but whenever we wanted dance, we go to Mary's. That's why I am here today to take class." Joe Cino was another company member, who later opened the Café Cino on Cornelia Street in New York City.

Walter Terry reviewed the December 13 premiere performance in the New York *Herald Tribune*. Overall, he concluded that it was a good program. The high points were *Trio* and *Threnody*. He thought *Songs* was "first class." Of *Threnody* Terry wrote,

Threnody, based on the Synge drama, *Riders to the Sea*, was rich in atmospheric power and sheer dance inventiveness. Miss Anthony captured in her scheme of action not only the element of lamentation but also the restless fear of waiting women and the sea's remorseless call to the men. The movements of the male figures were big and bold and the choral attitudes of the women as well as their individual excursions into hope or terror or despair were realized through actions almost classical in mold, classical in the sense of the antique theater.

Terry loved Anneliese Widman's performance in *Trio*. He wrote,

…exceptionally stirring was the dancing of Miss Widman. The choreographer had given her the choicest passages and had, it seemed to me, exploited the unusual gifts of this young artist more effectively than some other choreographers had done in the past. At any rate, Miss Widman moved through her measures with a sweeping flow of action, impeccable controlled, which made one gasp. The command was virtuosic but the treatment was pure poetry.

Besides Anneliese, the other dancers in *Trio* were Mary and Louis McKenzie.

In January of 1957, a review appeared in the *Dance Observer* that gave an outstanding review of *Threnody*. Critic Louis Horst deemed the premiere "…an exciting event of prime importance to the modern dance world." He thought *Threnody* was "…the most beautiful and complete dance composition this observer has seen in many a season," that it was "something approaching perfection." Horst was moved by the depth of Mary's "overwhelmingly human" choreography and her "powerful use" of props—in particular the rope and the black scarves the mourning women wore.

He also complimented the Bennington College Dance Group in *Threnody*, giving special mention to Bette Shaler for "…being especially moving as the mother" and Paul Bernsohn for "portraying the doomed son with great dignity." Horst felt that the work *Songs* suffered by following *Threnody* in the program. *Aperitif* opened the performance, and Horst relished in Mary's "…rare gift of this type of modern *commedia*." He thought the work was "…contagiously enticing, and saturated with the tart flavor of a double-martini." Of the dancers, he loved all five in this work: Alice Uchida, Louise McKenzie, Don Price, Joseph Cino, and Angelo Lo Vullo.

For Horst, the score from Benjamin Britten added dimension to this dramatic work. He wrote, "There is no doubt that Benjamin Britten's marvelous score adds a further dimension to *Threnody*, but it is equally true that *Threnody* adds a great one to Britten's music."

Years later Mary learned that Britten had composed his "Sinfonia" as a memorial for his mom and declared that it should never be danced. "When Miss Anthony learned that, she was appalled, for *Threnody* had been a success and she thought her dance was in no way disrespectful to the score," wrote Jack Anderson a 1980 the New York *Times* article titled "The Mary Anthony Approach." He continued, "She wrote a heartfelt letter to Britten, complete with a description of the choreography, photographs of the production, and copies of the reviews. Britten replied, "I think that is what my mother would have wanted," and allowed her to continue using the "Sinfonia."[20]

Years before her company's premiere in 1956, an astrologer had told Mary that she was going to do something marvelous in 1956, but would not receive the acclaim until 1957. This did, indeed, happen. The concert was in December 1956, and the great review by Louis Horst came out in *Dance Observer* in January 1957. It was a glowing review, and was the beginning of a series of marvelous reviews especially about the work *Threnody*. As a result, the company began to receive invitations to perform in other venues.

In July 1957, the Mary Anthony Dance Theatre performed *Songs, Threnody, Dark Song, The Catbird Seat,* and *Blood Wedding* in the Jacob's Pillow 25th Anniversary Dance Festival.[21] The company once again received great reviews.

In the *Times Union* of Albany, New York on July 4, 1957, the reviewer wrote, "New to the Pillow was the company of ten young dancers from Mary Anthony Dance Theatre of New York, exponents of the modern school of interpretative dancing...grace, co-ordination and perfection was the hallmark of their finished work." On July 3, 1957, The *Springfield Union* wrote,

> Not the least important facet of the program is the Mary Anthony Dance Theatre, a group of eleven artists who offered two works in the modern idiom. First scene was soft *Songs*, a suite of lyrical pieces inspired by poems of William Blake and set to music of Debussy....It is a mood piece of fine sensitivity contrasting the softness of the feminine with the strength of the men....But it is *Threnody* that the company makes its best contribution to the evening. Based on Synge *Riders to the Sea* and choreographed to a turbulent score by Benjamin Britten, *Threnody* is a dance drama of the sea.....Miss Anthony's choreography is highly inventive and charged with appropriate dramatic tension....Tom Skelton designed the lighting which adds to the effectiveness of both works.

The New York *Herald Tribune* critic was impressed by "the beautiful, poignant and imaginatively conceived *Threnody*." The reviewer was also moved by the performance of all the dancers and especially Paul Berensohn, noting he "...was both physically vital, and dramatically touching, a truly impressive enactment." Additional compliments went to "...Bette Shaler as the bereft mother and by Miss Anthony, John Starkweather, Cameron McCosh, and the other supporting dancers."[22]

The *Waterbury American* critic was also impressed with the "...dancing performance of that moving play *Riders to the Sea*." He wrote, "Mary Anthony with her dance group, which is only two years old as a group, has brought freshness, grace, poignancy, and talent to the dance and may be expected to make a rich contribution to the modern dance."[23]

The *Berkshire Eagle* critic wrote glowingly of the work *Threnody*, said that in *Songs* the "patterns were pleasant, movements sweeping and authoritative and the stage was full of motion, especially tight slashing turns like spirals in space, with the company showing meticulous training."[24]

As a result of the Jacob's Pillow performances, the White Barn Theatre in Westport, Connecticut became interested in Mary's work. White Barn founder and director Lucille Lortel invited the company to perform their works from Jacob's Pillow and also gave Mary a challenge. First, she asked if Mary would choreograph Tennessee Williams' *Purification* and show it in its entirety to Tennessee Williams' agent Audrey Wood. Wood loved it and gave them the green light. On August 4, Mr. Williams came to see the performance of his one-act play being performed as a dance-drama. Mary had Louis Calabro, whom she had met at Bennington College compose a special score for this new work. *The Purification* is a poetic play about a brother and a sister who represent the heavens—the stars, the sun, and the moon. The rancher in the story represents the earth. As the brother and sister are inseparable, the rancher kills the young woman out of his jealously for the love that she has for her brother. Overcome with grief, the brother kills himself.

On August 18, 1957, the company appeared in New London, Connecticut, which was reviewed by New York *Times* dance critic Selma Jeanne Cohen. She wrote,[25]

> Mary Anthony's *Threnody*, based on Synge's *Riders to the Sea*, is a touching rendition of a poetic drama admirably translated into dance terms. She has avoided the pitfalls of literalism without sacrificing individual characterization. The portrait of the grief-stricken mother is especially memorable as, one by one, she sees her sons taken from her by the merciless sea. And her final resignation is poignantly expressed. *Threnody* was danced by Miss Anthony and her group with Bette Shaler giving an expert performance as the mother.

Later that same year, the company performed *Plaisanteries d'Amour, The Purification,* and *Songs* at the 92nd Street YM and YWHA on November 10. Walter Sorrell wrote in the Providence *Journal* on November 11, 1957, that *Songs* was "…a handsomely woven tale of innocence and experience told in movement language of pure lyricism." The performance was also reviewed by Walter Terry of the New York *Herald Tribune* on November 24, 1957. Walter Terry called the company "…one of the most enterprising groups in the modern dance field." Of *Songs*, Terry wrote that it was "first class," and of *Threnody*, Terry stated, "Miss Anthony turned out her finest work—indeed, it is one of the finest in dance—for here she used movement to convey the themes and the emotional colors of a specific drama."

In 1958, Mary choreographed *Blood Wedding* (based on Garcia Lorca's play) using the music by Chavez, *At the Hawk's Well* (based on the play by W.B. Yeats), *Action Without Words* (based on the play *Act Without Words*, a mime for one player, written by Samuel Beckett in 1956) and *The Catbird Seat* (based on the story by James Thurber) using the music by Bowles. Lorca's tragic play *Blood Wedding* was written in 1932. It centers on a bridegroom, bride, and her lover who she leaves with after marrying the bridegroom. It ends in the bloody death of the bridegroom and the lover. *The Catbird Seat* was written in 1942 and takes place in the 1940s. James Thurber, the author and baseball fan, got his title for the story from Red Barber, a famous baseball radio announcer, who sat in the catbird seat. In the catbird seat, one can see all. The story centers on two individuals—a man who is meticulous, quiet, and protects the filing department of his job and a woman who is loud and outlandish in her laughter and her comments who wants to eliminate the man. The story centers on their conflict and the ending resolution.

On January 28, 1958 the company performed *Aperitif, The Purification, Songs,* and *Threnody*. On February 22, 1958 at the Brooklyn Academy of Music Mary's company performed the same program as part of a Dance Series. The company consisted of the same dancers it did at its opening, with the addition of Deborah Jowitt, Bette Shaler, Judith Spector, Paul Berensohn, John Starkweather, and Ann Dunbar Williams. Returning to the White Barn Theatre on August 3, 1958, Mary's company performed *Trio, The Catbird Seat,* and *Blood Wedding*.

In the fall of 1958, Mary traveled by train to Boston one day each week to teach at the Dance Circle. Her classes concluded with a performance of her company in November 1958 at the Bardwell Auditorium in Wellesley, Massachusetts. The title of the review was "Mary Anthony and Dancers." Of *Blood Wedding*, Margaret Lloyd wrote,

> Of course the energetic torso and large-scale gesture of modern movement might look a little extreme in the spoken drama, but in the danced version they become the very substance of the dramatic idea.[26]

New York *Herald Tribune* critic Walter Terry reviewed concert that combined Mary's company with Murray Louis and company and soloist Jean Cebron that took place at the 92nd Street Y at the end of November. Mary's company performed *Blood Wedding*. In Terry's review, he recognized Mary's work as danced drama. He wrote, "Miss Anthony is something else again. Her dance springs from the pulse of the heart and courses outward into the drama of life. She and her dancers are of this world, and they dance of conflict, of contentment, of resignation and the degrees of emotion linking them." He was impressed at how she could translate literature into choreography, adding, "Miss Anthony's choreographic patterns match the Lorca words in poetic eloquence."[27]

On December 2, 1958, the company performed at the Theater de Lys, The Greater NY Chapter (Lucille Lortel, Artistic Director). They performed *Blood Wedding*, *The Catbird Seat*, and *Threnody*. On December 21, 1958, Walter Sorrell reviewed this performance for *The Providence Sunday Journal*. He wrote,

> Her *Blood Wedding* was the best dance translation of this drama of passion and vengeance so far. The first part of it was less inventive and eloquent than the middle and final section, which were forceful and strong in their articulation of fury and pain. Bette Shaler as the bride and Mary Anthony as the mother communicated the inescapability of Lorca's tragedy.

During Mary's concert dancing and choreography, some of the African-American dancers who danced for her were Donald McKayle, who was from Harlem; Xavier Francis, who was from Washington; Ronnie Aul, who was from Mississippi; and Louis McKenzie, who was from Connecticut. Louis eventually went to Sweden. Ronnie went with Mary to Italy to dance in her second Italian musical and ended up staying in Italy, where he met and married a Spanish girl named Carmen.

In 1958, the company was invited to perform at the Virginia Museum Theater. They were told they were not allowed to bring the two African-American dancers of her company. Although Mary grew up in a segregated town, she never believed that race mattered. Because the company needed work, Mary reluctantly agreed to their terms and took only part of her company. Years later, her company was asked to return. Not wanting to repeat what had occurred on their first visit, Mary wrote and told that either the whole company comes to Virginia or no one comes at all. Her stand went all the way to the Governor of Virginia, who considered the situation. Because no laws prohibited African Americans from performing in Virginia, he sent her a telegram inviting all of the company members. As such, the Mary Anthony Dance Theatre was the first integrated company to perform in Virginia.

In December of 1958 the company participated in an event directed by Doris Humphrey with the Murray Louis Dance Company and soloist Jean Cebron, which took place at the 92nd Street YM and YWHA. In a review by Walter Terry on December 7, 1958 in the New York *Herald Tribune* titled, "Variety in the Modern Dance," he wrote, "Miss Anthony is something else again. Her dance springs from the pulse of the heart and courses outward into the drama of life. She and her dancers are of this world and they dance of conflict, of contentment, of resignation and the degrees of emotion linking them." Of *Blood Wedding* Terry wrote "…the inherent of movement itself, provide greater impact than any spoken words can do." He goes on to say, "*Blood Wedding* is one of the newest in a series of danced dramas which Miss Anthony has created and is, I think, her most successful venture since her remarkably conceived *Threnody*."

In the spring of 1959, Mary collaborated with Marvin Silversher in a theater piece called *Dialogues*. This piece contained the history of jazz from the time that the African people first came to this country to the present day. The leads were Donald McKayle and Dan Wagner, along with the rest of Mary's company. Odetta sang and Dave Bruebeck and his quartet played. Eddie Dowling, a Broadway producer, subsequently wanted to produce the piece on Broadway. They performed at Duke University. Again, Mary was very nondiscriminatory in selecting the people with whom she worked.

In November 1959, Mary staged and choreographed the opera *Orpheo* with music by C.W. von Gluck for the Rockland Lyric Theatre in Piermont, New York. A review in the newspaper of Nyack, New York on December 1, 1959 by Mariruth Campbell noted, "Staging and choreography by Mary Anthony was excellent, reflection the somber tone of the piece with vivid portrayals of the horrors of the underworld."[28]

In late 1959, Mary lost her three of her best dancers to Martha Graham (Bette Shaler, Dick Kuch, and Paul Bernsohn). Devastated, she also understood their reasoning—she didn't have as much work for them as Martha could provide. In fact, despite the company's strong reviews, they weren't receiving many new bookings for performances. Mary gives Martha a lot of credit, because Martha asked Mary's dancers to ask for her permission to work for Martha. Martha told the dancers that "Would you ask Mary if it would be all right if you came and danced with me?" Mary said of course. With the loss of the three dancers for whom Mary cared the most, she released the rest of her company dancers. The problems of both running a studio and holding a company were weighing too hard on her. At the same time, she had received an invitation to teach and choreograph for Bellas Artes Company in Mexico. In the spring of 1960, therefore, she packed up and headed for Mexico, leaving others in charge of keeping her school running for the six weeks she would be away from New York.

When she arrived in Mexico, she learned that funds were only available for her to teach and not to choreograph as she had been promised. Still, she would make the best of it. In spite of the mix-up, Mary had a marvelous time teaching with this modern dance company and bringing discipline to them. Learning that the Mexican dance company was always late to class, she set the following precedent: on the first day, she told the company manager that class would start exactly at 11AM and to lock the door after that. On that first day, of the 24 dancers, only three were on time. The other dancers had planned on drifting in; when they couldn't get in, they became upset. By the third day, all 24 dancers were there at 10:45 AM, and they dedicated themselves to Mary's work for six weeks. By the end, the dancers gave Mary so many presents she could barely get them all onto the plane.

When Mary returned to the US, she was revived and ready to immerse herself in company work. Her company consisted of Harriet Clifford, Paul Berne, Lynn Donovan, James Gardner, Paula Leland, and John Starkweather. For their first booking on July 20-21, 1960, the Mary Anthony Dance Theatre performed at the Michigan State University Summer Session and Lecture/Concert Series. They performed *Threnody* as part of a lecture demonstration on the 20th, and the next day they premiered a new work to the music *Symphony for Strings* by Louis Calabro. *Antiphon* is Mary's reaction to the events of the turbulent times. The word antiphon is derived from the part of a religious service that consists of sung questions and answers. In this dance, the word means "anti-communication." In the piece, Mary questions the time and what the future holds, and a chorus of dancers answers her. The playbill contained the following poem:

> Love me because I am lost; love me that I am undone.
> That is brave; no man has dared this – not one.
> Be strong to look on my heart as others look on my face.
> Love me – I tell you it is a ravaged, terrible place. –Louise Bogan

During Mary's tour in Michigan, the company performed *Threnody* at the lecture demonstration. A review of the dance in *The State Journal* on July 21, 1960 by an author known only by the initials E.W. wrote, "This superb performance came in the third part of what had been programmed as a lecture demonstration on 'contemporary dance' by Miss Anthony and her company, but was unquestionably the program's greatest splendor."[29] Of Britten's music and dance, the reviewer wrote,

> For all its sadness, was ideally chosen—and amounted surprisingly to
> a fully acceptable dance version of the great Synge drama, seen in the

past, on the campus, in both operatic and play form. The moving poetic story of women—and men—struggling against the might and greed of the sea, in an Irish fishing village, was told by the ineffable charm and grace of human motion having perfect pantomimic and narrative power.

These days were full of travel and adventure for Mary. In the fall of 1960, the Italian producers for whom she had choreographed the Italian musicals, invited her to return and spend three months choreographing for the weekly television show *Canzonissima*, which was the equivalent to America's *Hit Parade* and featured the most popular songs of the day. When she arrived in Italy, she was greeted by 18 dancers from all over Europe who were ready to work, and many of them were men. Feeling daily practice was important, Mary taught them a modern class every day, and they continued to work on little projects each day as well. Mary began working each and every day and not waiting for the scenery, costumes, or other accoutrements to arrive. New sets and costumes were being built each week, and they usually weren't delivered until the Friday morning of dress rehearsal with the orchestra. The dancers worked nonstop until they did the live show each Saturday night at 10 PM. Mary didn't perform in these shows, as it was a full-time job just to choreograph.

When Mary finished in January, she decided not to leave the continent without visiting Greece; it was so close. Cameron had always told her, "If a place is close that you have always wanted to visit, just go. Otherwise, you will regret it for the rest of your life." She went and was glad she did. She found true beauty. "The light was piercing. The scenery was breathtaking. It was a place where there was only truth," she said after her return. It was such a change from the commercial work she had been doing in Italy that Mary realized why the Greeks wrote the kind of theater they did. Reenergized, Mary returned to the United States and devoted herself only to teaching. She didn't want the responsibility of the company. At this point, Mary wanted to teach dancers to explore the way they themselves moved and not to copy her. She returned with a new point of view.[30]

Soon, however, Mary realized that teaching was not enough—her creativity needed an outlet. So, she gathered her best dancers for an August 1961 premiere of her new work *Venus and Adonis - A Masque* to music composed by John Blow in 1682. The performances took place at The Rockland Lyric Theatre in Piermont, New York. Conducting was Jerry Bidlack, with costumes by Pegeen Daly and scenery by Ion Laskaris and Piero Colacicchi.

After this very productive period, Mary hit her lowest of her lows. The love of her life, Cameron McCosh, died suddenly on February 25, 1962 while on tour in Colorado. Cameron was doing the show *Bye Bye Birdie* and attended a cast party after a show. Walking to his hotel room, he fell in the snow but wasn't found until the next day. The hospital called Mary and told her Cameron had suffered hypothermia and had developed pneumonia. The doctor assured Mary that Cameron would recover, so she didn't make the trip to Colorado to see him. Three days later, however, he died.

Together, Mary and Cameron had wonderful times mixing fun, work, and love. His death was such a tragedy—he died far too young and at the top of his career. He was the true love of Mary's life. Much later, she had other relationships, but Cameron held that very special place in her heart. Fortunately for us, Mary and Cameron created a modern dance record together called *Music for Modern Dance*. The recording gives us the barest of hints of how beautiful his music was.

Now, Mary had to go on with her life as Cameron would have wanted her to do—lift her chin and take one step forward at a time.

Mary Anthony during rehearsal at her studio, photo by Claudio Campuzeno

Mary Anthony and Joseph in "Look Up and Live"

A Dancer's Journey "It All Started With A Lie" 81

Mary Anthony and Joseph Gifford in "Look Up and Live"

From "Look Up and Live", Anneliese Widman kneeling, Irving Burton in back of desk, and Joseph Gifford kneeling

Mary Anthony and Ross Parkes in "Threnody", photo by V Sladdon

Mary Anthony and Ross Parkes in "Threnody", photo by Otto M Berk

Mary Anthony and Ross Parkes in "Threnody", photo by Otto M Berk

Mary Anthony in "Threnody", photo by V Sladdon

"Threnody", photo by Craft

Mary Anthony in her choreography of "Songs", photo by Kenn Duncan

Mary Anthony in her choreography of "Songs", photo by Kenn Duncan

Mary Anthony in her choreography "Songs", photo by Alan D Haas

Mary Anthony and Cameron McCosh in "Blood Wedding", photo by Paul J Cefola

Cameron McCosh in "Blood Wedding", photo Paul J Cefola

A Dancer's Journey "It All Started With A Lie" 87

from "Blood Wedding", left to right - Jo Lechay, Mary Anthony, Rosemarie Yellen, and Carol Payne

from "Blood Wedding", left to right - Louis McKenzie, Harriet Clifford, Cameron McCosh and Bette Shaler

from "Blood Wedding", left to right - Cameron McCosh, Harriet Clifford, and Mary Anthony

rehearsal of "Blood Wedding", left to right - Bette Shaler, Louis McKenzie, Cameron McCosh, and Mary Anthony

Louis McKenzie and Bette Shaler in "Blood Wedding"

Louis McKenzie and Mary Anthony in "The Purification"

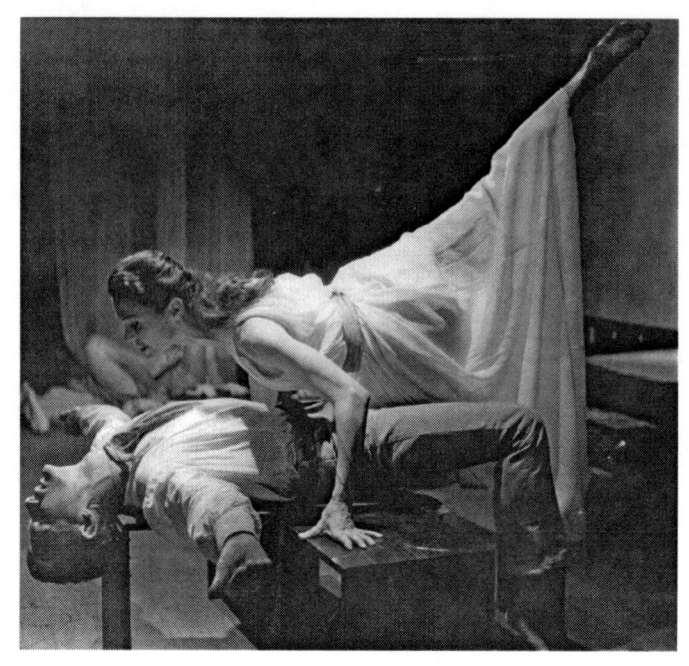

Mary Anthony and Cameron McCosh in "The Purification", photo by Alan D Haas

Mary Anthony and Cameron McCosh in "The Purification"

Mary Anthony and Louis McKenzie in "The Purification", photo by Burnice Schornfield

"At the Hawk's Well", left to right - Harriet Clifford, Mary Anthony, and Moss Cohen

"Antiphon", left to right - Daniel Maloney, Gwendolyn Bye, Michael Bruce, Muriel Cohen, Ross Parkes, and Tonia Shimin, photo by Lewis Brown

Daniel Maloney in "Antiphon", photo by Kenn Duncan

A Dancer's Journey "It All Started With A Lie"

"Canzonissima"

CHAPTER 6

Hard Work through Trial and Error Pays Off

Recovering from the loss of Cameron made 1962 and 1963 difficult years for Mary, but she kept moving forward, because she knew that time would heal her loss. Teaching in her studio and designing workshops with Jenny Eagan were creative outlets that gave her time to recover from her heartbreak. She had been incredibly prolific during her time with Cameron, but she would not produce any major new works in the years of grieving that followed his death. Ironically, this was when the world started opening up to her—Mary would finally gain the recognition in the United States and abroad that she had worked so hard to achieve.

At the end of 1962, Mary collaborated with Eagan, a professor at New York University's Department of Dramatic Arts, to develop a workshop dance course for actors who had little or no dance training. The course was called Dance-Drama Workshop. Classes were introductory and exploratory in nature and gave the actors a new sense of using their bodies on stage. They also focused on a stretching process for ease and flexibility. On December 19, the semester culminated with a performance at the First Presbyterian Church on 12th Street and 5th Avenue titled *Hegge-Wakefield Nativity*. The show's playbill said, "Without the fullest development of the individual personality in all its aspects, there is no art." Despite being beginners, the students gave the performance everything they had, infusing it with a special kind of power. The workshop was so successful that Mary and Jenny held another the following spring. That semester's production, called *The Trojan Women*, was held on May 7, 1963 at the Eisner Lubin Auditorium.

In August 1963, Mary choreographed and performed *A Winter's Tale* for the New York Shakespeare Festival at the Delacorte Theater in Central Park. A few months later, Mary entrusted her studio to company members and she returned to Paris to visit her dear friend Laura Sheleen, who had opened her own school in Paris just that year. When Mary and Laura reunited, it was like no time had passed since they had last been together. It's like that with close friends; you just pick up where you left off. Mary wanted to return to where she and Cameron had lived while working and living in Paris. Laura and Mary thus went to 68 Rue de Clamart just outside the City. When they arrived and knocked on the door, a French African boy peered through a tiny window in the door. Mary identified herself and asked to see the Madame. The young man said he had heard all about her from the Madame, who spoke often of Mary. Unfortunately, the Madame wasn't there; instead, Mary and Laura asked to see the garden, a place that held so many wonderful memories. Mary and Cameron often sat in the garden and dreamed under the fig tree. Now, the garden was overgrown with weeds, but the table and two chairs were still there. The young boy told Mary that when she and Cameron had left to return to the states, the Madame had suspended her daily gardening. It was sad, in a way. Mary didn't realize how much influence she and Cameron had in that charming house. Because Mary didn't get to see the Madame, she left a "little note" for her (Mary loves to call things "little"), saying that she was really disappointed that she missed her. Missing the Madame on Mary's visit only added to her realization that life moves on and changes.

Before leaving Clamart, she and Laura went to all the spots that Mary and Cameron had adored. To her happiness, the little bakery and the butcher shop were still there, just as she remembered them. What would have happened if she had stayed in Paris with Cameron? What if their child had survived? Mary always calls her aspiring students her children. And for her, they are.

By the end of 1964, Mary was feeling more alive again. Her school had been open for 10 years at this point, and the March 1965 article that Josephine Fox wrote in *Dance Magazine* brought even more students to the studio. The article explored Mary's rationale for her classes and choreography. "There are three kinds of theater," Mary told Fox. "There is the theater of entertainment—the circus, the Rockettes, the colorful folk dance companies, and of course, Broadway musicals. There is the theater that informs—Ibsen, the new young English playwrights. And, there is theater that illumines—Shakespeare's and the Greeks'—a theater that unfolds life and at the same time heightens it. It is that kind of theater that I have always aimed for in my choreography—the theater that illumines." Fox articulated this goal of illumination by adding, "She talks about 'focus' of the dancers' eyes. Her intention is to objectify what Stanislavsky calls 'communion' or 'spiritual intercourse' with the dancer's gaze of the eye. The eyes of the actor, as tiny as eyes are, are magnets for the audience. They hold attention. They reveal motivations."[31]

Mary also spoke with Fox about her unique system of choreographic workshops, which covered a two-year cycle. She taught three courses each year, which met for two-hour sessions after technique classes. The courses divided into six categories:

Classic. Mary emphasizes "focus," which she divides into three categories: "in focus," "contact focus" and "out focus." "In focus" is a gaze that is no more than three feet in front of you. Additionally, the dancer looks within. "Contact Focus" is communication with the audience, a performer or an imaginary person. "Out focus" is projecting focus outward beyond infinity.

> **History of Dance.** Here Mary emphasizes style—Primitive, Egyptian, Hindu, Greek, and Roman. The dancers explore the people of these historic periods—their thinking, living habits, the way they moved.
> **Medieval Period.** Here Mary and her students explore the way people moved during the Middle Ages.
> **Renaissance.** The dancers study Arbeau's *Orcheosographie* as well as 15th and 16th century dances.
> **Modern Forms.** This variation on the classic course uses contemporary music and builds simple group forms.
> **Drama and Dance.** This course focused on mime, acting, dance, and experiments with the movement and spoken word.

Mary explained her workshop goals to Fox. "Although the creation of movement is the ultimate end of this workshop," wrote Fox, "the emphasis on stretching the imagination helps the dancer to become a more creative performer."

When Fox's article appeared, dancers remained loyal to one studio. In contrast, years later, Mary lamented the trend that she calls "studio hopping." But even by the time Mary spoke to Fox, she was noticing a change in the number of classes a dancer took each day. She told Fox, "It amazes me today when I hear dancers exclaiming about how many classes they have had in one day, running through quantity is what they're after. There was a vitality in dancers then that I don't see today. And in all the young people—not just dancers—the careless, sloppy teenagers. In their gate there is no commitment to life. The way they slouch and round their spines, they show an 'I don't care' attitude about life. They have no dignity."

According to Mary, one who creates is rich. Fox expressed Mary's approach: "It suddenly became vividly clear that for her [Mary] to dance is to listen, to dance is to taste, and smell, to dance is to see and love. It is to be so full of life, so keenly aware, that the body overflows with its abundance of experience. It is an inner proclamation that one makes outwardly with the body."

Like Fox, writer and critic Jack Anderson summed up Mary's work calling it "The Mary Anthony Approach" in the New York *Times*. In his article, Anderson quotes Mary Anthony as saying, "The Contraction in modern dance is as major a discovery for us as that of the fifth position was centuries ago." He talked about Mary's experience when she came to New York City for the first time and went to an astrologer. The seer predicted that Mary's life would always be in theater and education, which came to be. Anderson said,[32]

> She fashioned a pedagogical approach that amalgamates elements of two major modern techniques: Martha Graham's and the Central European, as exemplified by Miss Holm, who in turn, was influenced by Mary Wigman and Rudolf von Laban, the Hungarian born theorist. Discussing these techniques, Miss Anthony said, 'Both can produce finished dancers. But in the Laban method you explore, explore, and explore movement problems until you finally solve them, whereas in the Graham method you repeat, repeat, and repeat a phrase until you have perfected it. From Laban you gain an awareness of space as a living thing; from Graham, a centering of the body. I give my students long dancey combinations in space that may reflect my Holm background. But I also teach contraction and release. The contraction can't be ignored.

Anderson noted, too, that Mary Anthony does not just teach dance technique; she teaches her students so much more. He said,

> She also directs what she calls the Creative Workshop, a composition workshop that is attended by actors, as well as dancers. In this workshop, Miss Anthony emphasizes structured improvisation and gives students dramatic problems to solve through movement. Many of the exercises derive from her translation of Konstantine Stanislavski's acting theories into dance terms. 'I often tell compositions students', Miss Anthony said, 'that if you know who you are, when and where you are, what you are doing there, and why you are doing it—Staniolavski's five Ws—your dance is already half made. I also want students to become aware of the possibilities of focus. You know you can change the entire quality of a movement by changing the focus of your eyes.'

Anderson goes on to quote Mary when he wrote,

> 'So few modern dance schools bother with composition nowadays. Today, it's nothing but technique. But when I was studying modern dance, technique was seen as a means to an end—and that end was always creative expression. That's why we studied more than technique alone. At Hanya's studio, for instance, Norman Lloyd taught music theory, Henry Cowell taught percussion and there were regular composition assignments. We were all eager to learn about the other arts, whereas some of today's kids are what Anna Sololow calls culturally deprived.'

Of her creative work, Anderson said, "Much of Miss Anthony's own choreography is a personal response to music that she has felt deeply. She has also based dances upon literary or dramatic themes."

During the mid-60s, Mary's company started getting more work. On April 23, 1965, the company was hosted by The Virginia Dance Society in a show titled *An Evening of Irish Theatre in Dance and Drama*, which Mary directed. The company performed *At the Hawk's Well*, *Action Without Words #2*, and *Threnody* from their repertoire. Although the audience was small for the performance, they were thrilled and appreciative.

Following the performance, a review appeared in the Richmond Times by Frances Wessels.[33] Wessels wrote, "It was a production of real artistic merit." Of *The Hawks Well*, he wrote, "It was magnificent theater." Also, of *Action Without Words #2*, he said, "The second dance was a complete turn-about—a gem of hilarity and charm. This dance came from a short paragraph by Samuel Beckett about a brooding man. This was Mary Anthony's starting place, and what ensued showed an imagination, wit, and sense of humor that was the delight of the evening." Wessels considered *Threnody* "…the strongest work of the evening." Overall he said, "The dancers of the Mary Anthony group were well trained in dance and acting, and the result was arresting drama and beauty."

In the summer of 1965, the company performed in Logan, Utah. Following the performance on July 31, there was a review in the *Herald-Examiner* by Zetta Peterson. Peterson said "Mary Anthony in her modern interpretation of the *Wind*, was the wind, moving with freedom and a variety of expressions. Her second number, *Soledad*, showed the masterful way that modern dance can set its own stage for incorporating dance steps and attitudes of a particular country, then poignantly reveal a lonely, tragic, Spanish woman. A striking red and black costume and unusual lighting added interest."

Tom Skelton was her lighting designer, and he wrote an article in *Dance Magazine* in which he talked about the solo and how he designed his lights. By e.e. cummings the subtitle for the poem *The Wind* is "imagine you are a house around which I am the wind." Tom Skelton said,

> By now I have come to realize that the 'house' of the narration is the center of the stage, and that the movement of the dancer covers only the area outside of the house. The open lyric style of the movement indicates that she is the 'wind' outside the house, but it is punctuated by dramatic gesture that shows that something inside the house is motivating the action. She is more than the wind blowing around a house, she is the outsider who doesn't belong, or she is the woman rejected by her lover, or she is the mother watching the child whose growing pains she cannot ease, or anything the imagination cares to associate with the dance.[34]

On November 6, 1965 Mary's company performed their show *An Evening of Irish Theatre in Dance and Drama* in Milwaukee, Wisconsin at the

Society of Fine Arts of Alverno College. Included in this tour was a master class taught by Mary. The Milwaukee *Journal* critic Walter Monfried (who considered Mary "...an accomplished and imaginative leader of modern dance in New York) wrote, "This is an unusual troupe in that its members are not only skillful dancers, but can recite English poetry with facility."

Returning to New York, the company participated in *Dance Theatre Workshop's* "Monday's at 9" program series. On November 15 and 22, 1965 they performed *At the Hawk's Well* and *Threnody*.[35]

In April 1966, the company performed *Plaisanteries D'Amour, Songs*, and *Threnody* at the State University at Buffalo, New York. Ruth Shapiro wrote a review in the newspaper *The Spectrum*. Of *Threnody*, Shapiro said, "Mary Anthony was moving as the mother...," and goes on to say, "The overall feeling of the program was one of synthesis. Fine choreography, good themes and dancers, added technically to broader effects. The unifications of heaven and earth, and completeness of circles seemed to be prominent themes. The pulling up from the stage and the pulling down from the ceiling, the circle of six people acting in a unit, and turns in circles created a 'wholeness in space.' Shapiro also commended Mary's dancers: "...A pleasing company of manly dancers and womanly women...created harmonious moods and meaningful communication with the audience."

From 1966–1969 Mary was invited to teach for several weeks at the annual Tanglewood Festival outside of Boston. Part of her residency included having her company perform the last week she was there. Her good friend Joseph Gifford coordinated these appearances.

The strong reviews kept coming. A Washington *Post* reviewer wrote, "...all have finely attuned ears that listen to the music. Their movements reflect this in the finesse and subtlety achieved nuances of a rewarding performance...everything is strong and nothing superfluous enters anywhere." A Cleveland *Plain Dealer* reviewer wrote, "The dancing was both lyric and dramatic in style and the dancers were excellent." For *Oberlin Review* of Oberlin College, the reviewer wrote, "Mary Anthony was definitely within her own medium as she generated great emotional feeling within the simple and subtle movement choreography."[36]

By this time, Mary had the reviews she needed to secure continued bookings for the company. They had been a long time coming, but through her tenacity, she finally persevered. This critical acclaim provided a launch pad for new achievements in the coming years.

"A Winter's Tale", Mary Anthony on the right, photo by Keith Staulcup

Mary Anthony teaching, photo by Brooks Kamaroff

Mary Anthony in "The Wind", photo by Peter Basch, Basch LLC

Louis McKenzie in "Plaisanteries", photo by Alan D Haas

"Plaisanteries", left to right - Better Shaler, Judith Spector, Joy Gitlin, photo by Alan D Haas

"Plaisanteries", left to right - Paul Berenshorn, Alice Uchida, and Cameron McCosh, photo by Alan D Haas

CHAPTER 7

The Golden Years

*I*n 1968, Mary' school was 14 years old and her company was 12. All her hard work was finally paying off. She began getting more performing engagements and choreographic opportunities. Companies from the United States and abroad, including Bat-Dor in Israel and the Pennsylvania Ballet, wanted her renowned work in their repertory. Her work was finally becoming known, just as her friends had assured her it would. Because she had all these years to explore and find her own dance language with her students, Mary's choreography really had the "Mary Anthony look." One could tell when Mary had trained a student or a company member. Mary's technique is lyrical, strong, sensitive, and not only incorporates space around the dancer, but also uses the dancer's interaction with the earth energy from the ground. Her technique has a simultaneously expressive, fluid, and percussive use of the arms and torso. For example, Mary's arms may do swirls and spirals while the torso undulates. And, all of this might happen during a high extension or big jump. At the same time Mary's choreography portrayed the thematic source of her inspiration.

Touring for established companies became much easier in 1965 when the U.S. government created the National Endowment for the Arts Touring Program, which included a pilot program called "Artists in the Schools." Mary and her company were among the first to participate in the two-week program to enter various grade levels of public schools for classes, lectures, and demonstrations. Then, as the program grew more successful and longer in length, Mary was offered more booking dates. Before the National Endowment for the Arts Touring Program, most small modern dance company members were only paid for performances, requiring that they earn their main income by waiting tables, doing secretarial work, or teaching. Now they could earn most of their income performing.

With the additional income and work, Mary added a few more dancers to her company. Before this burgeoning, the company consisted of nine to ten dancers. Now she was expanding to 13 and 14 dancers. These were the golden years, or as Mary calls them, "the glory years," for her company. All the dancers in Mary's company were excellent; among them, Mary particularly prized three.

Daniel Maloney was one of the first to join Mary during this prosperous time. After graduating from Ohio State University, he moved to New York City. His introduction to dance was seeing dance performances in Central Park, and he thought, "I can do that." At the university, he had been a runner, and he was in excellent physical condition. In 1965, Daniel came to study with Mary and joined her company in 1967. Like many of Mary's dancers, he also joined the Martha Graham Company and was a soloist in both companies.

One year after Daniel Maloney arrived at Mary's, in 1966, Ross Parkes joined the company. Mary found Ross quite by accident. One of the male dancers in Mary's company was unable to continue dancing, as he was leaving New York. He reassured Mary that he would find a replacement, and Ross Parkes was his choice. Ross was already dancing in the Pennsylvania Ballet doing mostly classical ballet, but his real love was modern dance. Telephoning Mary, Ross said he wanted to see her class and her choreography before he made a commitment. True to his word, Ross came and observed class and rehearsal and was moved by her work.

Ross Parkes was originally from Australia, where he began his performing career with Robert Pomie's short-lived company called Ballet Theatre Le Francais in Sydney. From Australia, he moved to London, appearing in *My Fair Lady*. In London, he received a scholarship from Martha Graham and moved to New York City to train with her. Two years later, in 1965, he entered the Martha Graham Company and in 1966, he joined the Pennsylvania Ballet and the Mary Anthony Dance Theatre. All three companies wanted Ross and worked around his schedule such that he could work with them all at the same time for many years.

Another gorgeous dancer who danced with Mary Anthony was Yuriko Kimura. A native of Kanazawa, Japan, she had performed with the Tokyo Ballet, performing title roles in *Coppelia*, *Ondine*, and *Orpheus and Euridice*. In 1966, she won a Fulbright Scholarship to study with Martha Graham; she later became a dancer in the Martha Graham Company. Because Martha's company was not always active, she joined Mary Anthony's company in 1969.

With Ross Parkes, Daniel Maloney, Yuriko Kimura, and other professional dancers under her wing, Mary enjoyed this very creative and productive time with the company. When Martha's company became active again, the dancers would work with her, because she gave them more work. Mary worked around Martha's schedule; that way, they could still dance for Mary, too. Mary particularly loved working with Ross and Yuriko, as their concentration was so total. They took what Mary had given them and worked it out on their own. The next time Mary saw them, they gave a deep performance of the material. With Daniel, Mary gave him the opportunity to choreograph, because he always had so many choreographic ideas. In contrast, when the dancers worked with Martha, she would teach them her steps rather than letting them explore creative ideas.

At this point, Mary was branching out and setting her work on other companies. In the late 60s, Mary set *Threnody* on the Pennsylvania Ballet and was invited to teach and choreograph for several weeks for the newly formed Bat-Dor Company at the Batsheva Institute located in Tel Aviv, Israel. In 1967, Baroness Bethsabee de Rothschild established the Bat-Dor Dance Company for Jeannette Ordman, a classical ballet dancer from South Africa who captured the heart of the Baroness. Ordman was the artistic director, principal dancer, and headmaster of its dance school. From the beginning, Bat-Dor's style was a combination of modern dance with a strong emphasis on the technique of classical ballet. The Baroness gave generous financial support to Bat-Dor, making it possible for the ensemble to purchase the works of important artists from all over the world. And, Mary was one of those artists.

Mary set *Songs* and her new piece *Antiphon* on the Bat Dor-Company. When she was in Israel, Ordman was in Paris. When she returned, Mary had completed setting *Songs* and *Antiphon*, both of which were welcomed in the repertory of the company.

Seeing Israel for the first time was amazing to Mary. She was so impressed by how this tiny country had literally, as she said, "torn a living out of the desert." Mary said the farmland was created out of the desert using irrigation methods that implemented a special technique that doesn't lose water. Mary marveled that the Israeli side of the road was dotted with lemon and orange trees, schools, buildings, and plumbing, in drastic contrast to the Palestinian side of the road, where the people were living as if it was 5,000 years ago, with mud huts and no plumbing. On Sundays, her day off, Mary visited different places such as Yad Vashem, Jerusalem, and other towns in Israel.[37]

In the years that Mary left her studio to travel, teach, and choreograph, communication was very difficult and slow. Long distance by telephone in the United States was expensive and exorbitant to call another country. As such letters were the only communication channel for Mary when she was abroad. Letters could take two- to six weeks to reach another country. When Mary went overseas to work, she always left the studio with someone she could absolutely trust to run it without her.

So, when Mary returned to New York from Israel, she was shocked to learn that the building housing her studio had changed hands, and the new landlord wanted the floor her studio occupied to rent to a higher paying tenant. There was no convincing him, even though she pleaded. After many months of searching, she had looked at every available loft, from 24th Street down to Houston on the lower East side; indeed, everything was too expensive. One of her devoted students, Liz Aaronson, saw an ad in the New York *Times* for a loft located at 736 Broadway on the 7th floor. Mary and Ross Parkes went and looked at it just before Thanksgiving. At one time it had been a little theater, but by now it was dirty and run down. It had been rented by six Midwestern men who one-by-one became involved with film and television. There was only one of the men left holding down the fort, so to speak. Mary wanted this place, but she needed to move in and have it opened by December 1, 1969 when her other lease expired. Mary, Ross, Patrick Suzeau, and Theresa Reynolds worked night and day to get the place ready to open on December 1. All the money that Mary had made in Israel and the Pennsylvania Ballet—a mere $3,000—went to renovating her new studio. At first, Mary hated this new space, because she was really attached to her old space where she lived and worked. Furthermore, she had been at the original studio for 15 years. But as time wore on, she realized that the new space was lighter and airier.

Between 1968 and 1970, the company performed in many higher education facilities—the University of Massachusetts; Colby College in Waterville, Maine; Boston University Tanglewood Institute; and Oberlin College in Cleveland, Ohio. At that point, the cost to book the Mary Anthony Dance Theatre was $10,000 per week for up to seven performances. A single performance at a college was $2,000, plus transportation and accommodations. Two performances were $3,000 plus expenses. A lecture demonstration was $500, and a master class was $150. These figures were based on a company of 10 to 14 dancers. For a company of five to seven dancers, the cost was available on request.

The company appeared at the University of Massachusetts at Bowker Auditorium in October 1968. They opened the program with *Antiphon*, and her classics *Songs* and *Threnody*. In April 1969, her company performed the same repertoire at Colby College in Waterville, Maine. In August 1969, the company danced at Boston University's Tanglewood Institute and presented *Aperitif, The Pursued, Antiphon,* and *Songs*.

In late 1969, Mary worked with Ross Parkes to create the first section of her work *In the Beginning*, which she named "Adam," again drawing her inspiration from the Bible. Mary had wanted to choreograph this work for a long time, and now she had a dancer for whom she wanted to create it. She had already selected her music, titled *Sun Music I*, composed by Peter Sculthorpe. At the same time, she was working with her company on a new work, *Gloria*, to music by Francis Poulenc. Against the futility of the Vietnam War, Mary choreographed this work as an affirmation of life. It had been several years since she had created new choreography. After Cameron's death, Mary had been in a creative slump and mostly taught, guest taught, or set established works on other dance companies. And with time, by 1968 and the addition of Ross Parkes, Yuriko Kimura and Daniel Maloney, her spirit was reborn.

In January 1970, Mary did a three-week engagement at Oberlin College in Cleveland, Ohio that culminated with two performances of her company. For the three weeks she taught modern dance classes to college students, sharing her specialized approach. The company presented two premieres: *Gloria* and Ross Parkes' solo "Adam." The company also performed *Aperitif, Threnody,* and Horton's *Dedication to José Clemente Orozco.* After the Oberlin College performances, reviewer Eleanor Frampton of *The Plain Dealer* wrote,

> The dancing was both lyric and dramatic in style and the dancers were excellent when the Mary Anthony Dance Theatre was presented by Oberlin College in Hall Auditorium. Miss Anthony sticks firmly to her credo that the human body is the instrument of dance and can be used to express the ideas and emotions of people. She makes the attempt to shock the audience, deafen it or give it double vision, but relies on dancing for any impact.[38]

Like many other reviewers, Frampton felt the high point of the program was *Threnody*. She was impressed with Mary's ability to portray tragedy in the role of the mother. For Mary's choreography of *Gloria,* Frampton wrote, "Miss Anthony's choreography was tightly knit with interesting patterns and technical variations which at moments achieved an ecstatic quality." Mary's work *Aperitif* opened the performance, of which Frampton wrote, "*Aperitif* was just that, an amusing bit of whimsy to whet the appetite…The group took on added luster when Miss Anthony appeared with it. She gave it maturity and focus."

In the summer of 1970, Mary completed another part of *In the Beginning*, which she titled "Eve," a duet with Ross Parkes and the beautiful dancer Yuriko Kimura. Loving the music of Sculthorpe, Mary used his *Sun Music III* to complete this section of her choreography. *In the Beginning* would ultimately become one of her more signature pieces.

Later that fall, Mary's company had two engagements at the Fashion Institute of Technology Theater. This would be their first New York engagement in several years, because they had spent so much time touring. At these performances, she premiered *In the Beginning*: "Eve" and her work in progress *Dream Flight* with music by Luigi Nono. *Antiphon* and *In the Beginning*: "Adam" were New York premieres for the company. They also performed Mary's signature work *Threnody* and James Truitte's staging of Lester Horton's choreography *To Jose Clemente Orozco* to music from Kenneth Klaus. *To Jose Clemente Orozco*, a duet, is one of Horton's five *Dedications in Our Time,* originally created in 1953. Excellent reviews followed the Fashion Institute show. On October 15, 1970, a review appeared in *The Village Voice* from critic Deborah Jowitt (who danced in Mary's early company). She wrote,

> To work with Mary Anthony is to love her. Another thing: her movement feels so good on your body. It's full and open and ought to be beautiful. I'm not the only one to notice this; dancers who performed in her concert last weekend said they felt that way too…Her moving *Threnody* has always worked in that its theme (it's based on Synge's *Riders to the Sea*) is compatible with those smoothly surging dance phrases. The rhythms of the sea—whether angry or peaceful—hold the dance together. It also succeeds because Mary Anthony has a real sense of the play and knew just how to translate it into dance. She herself performed the role of the bereft mother with immense power. Ellen Robbins as the younger daughter and Ross Parkes as one of the sons were especially good. I thought, at the kind of dance—acting that *Threnody* requires…*Dream Flights*, a work in progress, has a smooth, gliding, and spinning feel to it.

Of "Eve" Jowitt wrote,

> [It was] a pure pleasure to watch. Also, Anthony has a fine sense of dramatic timing in works that require it; she knows just how long a particular mood or moment ought to last.

Mary felt that it was important that her company perform other choreographers' works, especially famous historical pieces. *To José Clemente Orozco* was such a work. Jowitt wrote,

> I'd seen it years ago when Alvin Ailey and Carmen de Lavallade performed it, and Daniel Maloney and Tonia Shimin stacked up surprisingly well against that memory. Maloney had the solidness, Shimin the courageousness that the dance needs.

Another review appeared in New York *Times* on October 12, 1970 titled, "Anthony Troupe Gives Premieres Retelling of Adam and Eve Legend Best of Group" by Anna Kisselgoff. She appreciated the broad range of quality works that the company performed. Of Mary's premiere work *In The Beginning*, she wrote, "Miss Anthony has constructed a striking piece, expressive in its movement and subtle in its theme." Of "Adam," Kisselgoff wrote,

> [It] consisted of a solo magnificently danced by Ross Parkes, which conveyed all of the terror and self-definition of a being who discovers he is first man on earth. Although one of Miss Anthony's initial images

came straight from Michelangelo's *Creation of the World*, it was a fully original piece—from Mr. Parkes first colt-like staggering through his growth from beseeching dependence upon God to an image of independence, suggesting free will. In "Eve," the other section, Yuriko Kimura joined Mr. Parkes in a psychologically nuanced duet that created its effect through suggestion rather than statement.

The Fashion Institute performances also spurred other strong reviews. *Dance News* reviewer Trudy Goth loved the versatility of the dancers and their technical skills along with their strong sense of stage presence. Like the other critics, Goth felt that Mary's work *Threnody* is a strong work. Goth wrote,[39]

> The highlight of the evening was *In the Beginning* consisting of two parts. A solo "Adam" well danced by Ross Parkes, conveyed the initial insecurity of the first human creature on earth. In the second part, "Eve," Mr. Parkes was joined by Yuriko Kimura whose appearance lit up the stage and made the whole evening eminently worthwhile. Her projection, technique, looks and personality created one of those rather infrequent moments of complete satisfaction and awareness that here is a talent to watch, a name not to be forgotten.

Dance Magazine critic Doris Hering wrote,[40]

> In Mary Anthony's dance metaphor men move like men; women move like women. It's a refreshing change in today's unisexual dance environment. The strength of that conviction warmed its way especially through her two part *In the Beginning*, which consisted of a solo for Ross Parkes as Adam and a duet for Parkes and Yuriko Kimura as Eve…The company has spirit and unity…It was a joy to see Miss Anthony herself as the mother [in *Threnody*]….The Mary Anthony Dance Theatre would be welcome on any touring circuit.

The Mary Anthony Dance Theatre performed again in December at the Fashion Institute. Mary premiered the third part of *In the Beginning* called "Cain and Abel" with music by Irkanda IV. And she did a New York premiere of *Gloria* with music by Francis Poulenc along with her classic *Songs*.

Of this performance, The New York *Times* critic Don McDonagh wrote,

> Two splendid reasons to see Mary Anthony Dance Theatre are Ross Parkes and Yuriko Kimura. Others are Daniel Maloney, Ellen Robbins, and Tonia Shimin. The choreography of the works they appear in has a friendly and craftsman like predictability that allows the dancers to appear to excellent advantage…Miss Kimura and Mr. Parkes … make

a striking impression coiling languorously around one another or spasming separately from the prod of guilt. She is lithe and quick, springing toward and away from him...He moves around with confidently assertive power...Miss Anthony knows the skills and abilities of her company and she choreographs knowingly to them.[41]

Another review in *Dance News*, in February 1971, was written by Walter Sorrell, who particularly enjoyed the complete trilogy of *In the Beginning*. Sorrell wrote,

> *In the Beginning* has its impressive and sometimes haunting moments. This work stands somehow in contrast to Miss Anthony's former choreography. As if *In the Beginning* were a new beginning for her she tries to explore new ways of expressiveness. They are dramatically intense as they are still traditionally structured, but with a difference. She believes in a beginning, middle and end—and in the sequence-returning with a heightened conclusion to the conceptual imagery of the beginning as in "Adam" and "Eve" [Part I and II].

Walter Sorrell could see her choreography changing and becoming freer in finding new forms of communication. Of *Songs* he commented on the turns, swinging gestures, which created "a warm sensuous, melodic feeling echoing Debussy's sensibilities." The work *Gloria* with music by Poulenc originally premiered at Oberlin College in January of 1970. For this New York premiere, Sorrel said "I particularly found this final section a rewarding experience. The entire ensemble—twelve very fine dancers—contributed its share to make the choreographer's intentions appear most spirited."

In March 1971, a lovely review of the December 1970 concert by Lothar Michners appeared in the German magazine *Das Tanzarchiv* and was translated into English by Aarmgaard Bartellanden. Michners stated,

> Miss Anthony's power is the dramatic presentation of the human being in relation to his surroundings. Reality of life becomes the leitmotiv of her choreography, which she masterfully points out in her analysis. This demands from her dancers as much acting as dancing. Miss Anthony knows how to make out of each of her dancers her perfect instruments. Mary Anthony can be compared with Martha Graham in that the relation of her concept and its execution both, transform choreography into a theatre piece which demands for the audience great concentration.

During the year 1971, Mary encouraged some of her company members to choreograph for the company. She wanted them to have an opportunity to create a work for a large venue. Even in the early days of the Mary Anthony

Dance Theatre, she included works of other choreographers such as Joseph Gifford and Lester Horton. Company members Muriel Cohan choreographed *Ooka the Wise* (music improvised and played by Elliot Weiss); Daniel Maloney choreographed *Reflections of Spoon River* and *Whiff Whiffle*; Ross Parkes choreographed the works *Inside of Him* to a song by Richie Havens and *1 2 3 4 5* ; and Marcia Plevin choreographed *Piece*. At this time, Mary was creating a Christmas nativity themed work, *A Ceremony of Carols* in ten parts, with music by Benjamin Britten. Mary had the costumes made especially for this work by Leor C. Warner II, an established costumer in New York for Broadway and dance. For the most part, the costumes were nativity period costumes that were made of lightweight fabric and flowed with Mary's choreography. The dancer portraying baby Jesus wore a white linen loin cloth costume, and the dancer portraying the angel wore a costume much like the angels in the paintings of Michaelangelo . The dancer portraying the spirit of joy* wore a long sleeved leotard with large piping around the shoulders and the upper thighs, with footed tights and no shoes.[42]

All of these works were performed over several weeks at the theater of the Riverside Church, located on West 120th and Riverside Drive in New York City. Many dance companies were performing at this theater, as the auditorium was sized perfectly for a modern dance audience, and the rent was only $600 per week, making it more affordable.

Following the new repertory performances, many nice reviews came out The New York *Times'* critic Anna Kisselgoff noted the choreography of Mary's company members. She wrote, "In general, the choreographers showed a tendency toward dramatic emphasis rather than pure dance, with some even turning to spoken narrative." Of the works, she found Marcia Plevin's choreography to be the strongest work on the program of new choreographers. Of Plevin's *Piece*, Kisselgoff wrote, "Her study of a couple that seemed to rid themselves of sexual hang-ups through a group encounter, was treated with forcefulness and professionalism."[43] Of *A Ceremony of Carols*, the New York *Times'* critic Don McDonagh said,

> The real pleasures offered by well-trained dancers along with precision and craftmansly care in choreography are always an integral part of the Mary Anthony Dance Theatre. On Monday evening at the Theater of Riverside Church the company offered a new work created by Miss Anthony, *A Ceremony of Carols*. The piece has particular relevance to the season but would exert its soft-spoken charm at most any time. Set to Benjamin Britten's *Ceremony of Carols*, it tells the story of the birth of the Christ child in ten brief scenes. The feeling of the piece is a quiet lyricism. By necessity it is as episodic as any collection of carols would

be but manages to string its incidents together smoothly for the most part. Among the dancers, Mary Price, Marcia Plevin, and Aaron Osborne were particularly noticeable.[44]

Of the entire mixed repertory performed, reviewer David Kerry Heefner wrote in *Show Business* (the weekly theatre publication), "In her choreography, Mary Anthony shows a flair for theatricality." Heefner said that Mary's works contained a special "audience holding power." He wrote, "This was due in part, I believe, to her use of contrast and variation, for she never bogged down in a mood or quality of movement, (as it often happens) and stayed there for an entire work, but changed the pace or feeling or focus at the right moment, creating new interest and tension, which added and built toward the climax."

Heefner was impressed with Mary Anthony's performance in her work *Gloria*. Of Mary's performance, he said, "Her appearance pointed up the importance of emotion to 'modern' dance, for everything she did had the added excitement of involvement and personalization. Each gesture, every turn of her head was precise and conveyed inner life and character."

A lovely review appeared in *Applause* magazine written by Nancy Bornstein. From the Riverside performance series, Bornstein found the most outstanding dancers were Mary Anthony herself plus Yuriko Kimura, Elisa Monte, and Ross Parkes. She also noted some of the new choreographers, when she wrote,

> In *1 2 3 4 5* Ross Parkes has created a three-part piece that has both strikingly beautiful and completely pedestrian moments. The first section, of five women, led by Gwendolyn Bye, is visually arresting. Miss Bye, (a pretty, round-faced blonde) wore the same white top and bell-bottomed trousers as the other women, with a belt of blue and white beads. The lighting was particularly effective – rays of light kept catching the gleam of Miss Bye's blonde hair, of Mary Price's red hair, of the soft flowing white material, as the dancers leaped and twirled in a circle, and in lines. The second section was more openly sensual. Three male dancers (Mel Jones, Daniel Maloney, and Patrick Suzeau) moved slowly and smoothly in and out of poses, performing involved gymnastic feats, naked save for abbreviated white trunks. Their bodies made fascinating shapes, and the even flow of the slow motions was almost mesmerizing…The final section of *1 2 3 4 5* is a duet with Elisa Monte, a small, dark-haired, extremely expressive dancer, and Daniel Maloney.

Of Ross Parkes' other choreography of the Richie Havens song, *Inside of Him*, Bornstein noted Yuriko's "beautiful control and special quality of lightness." This work was a love duet for Ross and Yuriko. She found the choreography of Daniel Maloney's *Whiff Whiffle* to be a very funny dance that for the most part worked. Of the piece, she said,

> It's a good television skit kind of dance, performed by dancers who are also fine comedians. The best bits include: Mary Price attempting a wobbly-legged pointe solo, dressed in a little girl's recital outfit—a gaudy pink tutu with a glittery tiara, and a trailing 15-or-so-foot organdy veil that gets in everybody's' way; Meryl Brownstein trying to dance while completely engulfed in a mass of balloons; Gwendolyn Bye as a drunken White Rock Soda Fairy; and (best of all) Elisa Monte as the Morton Salt Girl ("When it Rains, It Pours"), whose salt box refuses to corporate.

A Ceremony of Carols also got a good review in the *Chelsea Clinton News* by the critic Marion Sawyer. Sawyer wrote,

> In observance of the holiday Ms Anthony offered *A Ceremony of Carols* (Benjamin Britten) in ten short scenes with an exquisite suggestion of set by Thomas Munn. Attitudes and gestures were stylized after early Renaissance paintings and favored an iconic rather than realistic depiction of incidents associated with the nativity.

The company toured to Geneva, Ohio to perform and hold master classes and a lecture demonstration. After the company performed *The Pursued, Songs, In the Beginning:* (Parts 1 and 2: "Adam" and "Eve"), and *Threnody*, a lovely review appeared in *The Geneva Times* on May 4, 1972 titled "Theatre Group Illuminates Audience" by Douglas Tepper. Tepper marveled at the quality of the dancers and choreographic patterns, and he thought the company members were great actors, too. Tepper stated, "Miss Anthony's company is a synthesis of experienced dancers, particularly Jean Paul Comelin, Ross Parkes, and Yuriko Kimura and dancers of great, potential energy as Gwendolyn Bye and Linda Hayes. Also dancing were Mel Jones, Daniel Maloney, and Elisa Monte." Of these experienced dancers Tepper wrote, "In them, we see a marvelous feel for theatricality in her choreographic patterns and gestures, but beyond this we have a concentration of dance and acting. This is Mary Anthony's greatest achievement." Of *Songs*, Tepper said, "Here, we see an excellent balletic ensemble of Miss Kimura, Elisa Monte, and Linda Hayes. Once again Miss Anthony proved that the intricacy and complexity of lyrical movement can also stand alone as pure organic form. The three men, Jean Paul Comelin, Daniel Maloney, and Mel Jones, in limited roles, danced with masculine vigor doing especially exhilarating lifts." Of Ross Parkes and Yuriko Kimura in *In the Beginning*, Tepper said, "The appearance of Yuriko Kimura brought forth the best of Miss Anthony's goals. This excellent pairing choreographically understated, allowed them to perform as one, augmenting one another and becoming much more than two dancers."

In the fall of 1972, two of Mary's works were featured at the Anta Theatre at City Center American Dance Marathon, where they performed *In the Beginning* and Horton's *To José Clemente Orozco*. Many positive reviews followed, and one of note was written by Doris Hering in the February 1973 issue of *Dance Magazine*. Hering said,

> Mary Anthony is by no means a prolific choreographer, but everything she does turns out meticulously crafted. And she is not afraid to say what she really means, even at the risk of being unabashedly romantic, as in her duet In the Beginning... What I particularly liked about Miss Anthony's opening solo for Ross Parkes as Adam was its mystery and its immediate courage. Lying on his luminous disc, with frame forms behind him and with Peter Sculthorpe's clean-cut score building around him, you could feel the glow of Adam's vitality and mounting courage.[45]

On October 17, 1972 Clive Barnes reviewed this show for the New York *Times*. He wrote, The program opened with Miss Anthony's group in Lester Horton's *To José Clemente Orozco*. This duet, revived by James Truitte, has a lazy charm and style. It manages to suggest the painter and the time. I haven't seen this work in years—I recall it being danced by Joyce Trisler and Alvin Ailey. It has a pungent quality and was here eloquently danced by Tonia Shimin and Daniel Maloney.

Regarding *In the Beginning*, Barnes wrote "Miss Anthony is singing a song of innocence...The work starts with an expansive and sinuous solo for Adam, exceptionally well danced by Ross Parkes. In the second part, the beautifully controlled Mr. Parkes is joined in a duet by Yuriko Kimura. The dance has a radiant luminosity, and Miss Anthony's choreography had style and purpose."

In June 1973 the Mary Anthony Dance Theatre returned to do a series of mixed repertory performances at the Theatre of the Riverside Church. Of Mary Anthony's choreography, the company performed *Blood Wedding*, *In the Beginning*, and *Trio*. Other repertory pieces were Anna Sokolow's famous work *Rooms*, Daniel Maloney's *Reflections of Spoon River* and *Power*, Ross Parkes' *Inside of Him* and his adagio from *1 2 3 4 5*, and Muriel Cohan's choreography *Chamber Piece*. Ross Parkes' new choreography, *Tides*, was a lyrical piece depicting the ebb and flow of human emotions.

Reviews followed that complimented Mary Anthony's works as well as the work of the other choreographers. Clive Barnes' review appeared in The New York *Times* on June 24, 1973, titled "Ballet: A Haunting Work." Barnes paid Mary a great compliment by saying, "Miss Anthony, who has been running the company for close to 20 years now, is one of those second-generation of modern dancers who have played such a notable role in establishing the present technical and stylistic quality to be found in this field today." Of Anna Sokolow's *Rooms*, he wrote,

> Miss Kimura shines...The company, particularly its two leading dancers, Ross Parkes, who is also the associate director and Yuriko Kimura, is good, with a modest and harmonious style... Mr. Parkes showed a sharply defined neurotic power as a man in panic, and, finally, Miss Kimura was poignant and plaintive as a lonely girl contemplating suicide. This is a strange work about alienation caused by cities and the inhumanity of society. It does credit to the Anthony repertory.

Another famous New York *Times* dance critic, Anna Kisselgoff, recognized Mary Anthony's dancers as some of the best in the field. Kisselgoff said, "One good reason for attending the current brief season of the Mary Anthony Dance Theatre… is that two of its members, Yuriko Kimura and Ross Parkes, are among the most outstanding performers in modern dance today."[46]

Of the mixed repertory, Kisselgoff noted Ross Parkes' and Daniel Maloney works. Of Parkes she wrote, "The lesson of the evening turned out to be the durability of Mr. Parkes' two works from 1971. His Richie Havens love duet for himself and Miss Kimura, *Inside of Him*, with its slippery fish flow, and the adagio from *1 2 3 4 5*, with Ulysses Dove, Mr. Maloney, and Patrick Suzeau powerfully emitting the loneliness of men whose world resembles an asylum, are pieces that appear more impressive than previously." Of Maloney's work *Power,* she wrote, "It was a pleasant, mod tribal rite and showed Mr. Maloney's increasing choreographic deftness."

In September 1973, the Mary Anthony Dance Theatre toured to Orono, Maine to perform and hold master classes at the University of Maine. After returning to New York, the company performed again in October at the Fashion Institute of Technology. And the high point of the year was the performance of *Ceremony of Carols*, held on Christmas Eve, with the Broadway United Church of Christ Choir at St Paul the Apostle Church in the heart of the city.

On January 7-19, 1974 the Mary Anthony Dance Theatre did a two-week "Artists in the Schools" residency at two high schools in St Paul, Minnesota. The residency consisted of master classes, lecture demonstrations, teacher workshops, and a public performance, which brought a lovely review in *St. Paul Pioneer Press* by Jeff H. Harvey. Harvey loved *Threnody* with Mary Anthony dancing the role of the mother who loses her sons to the sea. Harvey says, "It is a work big in design and gesture, rich in inventiveness and contrast between masculine and feminine movement, direct in metaphor and powerful in impact...Consistently taut in line and admirably danced in both individual and group passages, the performance was further enriched by the achingly expressive work of Miss Anthony in the mother's role." He also loved the performance of Ross Parkes and Yuriko Kimura in *In the Beginning*, where he says, "These are absorbing dances, touching, sinuous and beautiful, delineating Adam's wonder and terror in his discovery of himself and the world, his loneliness, and the innocent sexuality of his and Eve's mutual discovery of each other and their humanness."[47]

Another review of the Minnesota performances compared Mary to Martha Graham, calling her work "neo-Martha Graham." The review was written by Mike Steele for the Minneapolis *Tribune* on January 15, 1974. Perhaps he compared her to Martha Graham because Graham's choreography is dramatic and intense, or perhaps because many members of Mary's company were also in the Graham Company. In any case, he wrote, "Like a lot of choreographers coming to the fore in the 1950s, Miss Anthony presents dance with an emphasis more on drama than pure movement, more on a soul-searching seriousness, an agonizing inner life than on humor or kinetic wit...As choreographer, Ms. Anthony is a superb craftswoman, always firmly in control of her space, always aware of the movement qualities of her company-very balletic, formal, tense and intense...it's good, solid, professional work...Her best works are expressive and thematic dance dramas." However, unlike Martha Graham, Mary incorporated other choreographers into her company repertory, her choreography is more fluid, and she is not the center around which all of her choreography is created. While Martha's choreography often dwells on a psychological moment that a character experiences, Mary's storytelling is more linear and forward moving.

Adding more famous works to her repertory in 1974, Mary had Charles Weidman reset *Fables For Our Time* on her company. Originally, Mary had performed this work at the Ziegfeld Theater in 1949 with the New Dance Group. Charles had received a grant to restage the work on Mary's company, but the grant only paid for the restaging. Mary's company dancers had to rehearse for free, because Mary had no money, not even for costumes. Mary and her dancers felt it was that important to do this highly acclaimed work.[48]

Because the work had not been done in a long time, and even before videotapes of choreography were made, Mary and Charles put their heads together to remember Charles' choreography. The two found it difficult to remember the original choreography, so Mary talked to Betty Osgood and Charles Morris, who had been a part of the Humphrey Weidman group. They, however, could only remember snippets as well. Betty reminded Mary that when Charles Weidman choreographed a work, he would have the dancers try different things, and together they would develop the material. This was difficult for the company that Mary had in 1974. They were more technique oriented, and they were accustomed to the steps being given to them. After the first rehearsal, however, they became comfortable working like this, were enchanted by Charles, and realized what a gift they were receiving. Weidman's charming work added wit to Mary's repertory. In fact, the first time the company performed the work was in October 1975 at the Marymount Manhattan Theatre. In The New York *Times* of March 12, 1989, Jennifer Dunning wrote that *Fables for Our Time* is a "goofy, witty evocation of James Thurber's musings on the human condition." Mary felt that Charles Weidman was significantly responsible for bringing much of the comedic timing to American modern dance.

In the spring, the company performed on March 21 at New York University performing Mary's *Songs*, and the "Adam" portion of *In the Beginning*. Additionally, they performed Sokolow's *Rooms*, and Maloney's *Power*.

On May 7, the company participated in the YM-YWHA's Modern Dance Retrospective performing *In the Beginning*. The company performed in Bay Shore, New York as part of the Brightwaters Library's Performing Arts Series on May 25, 1974. They performed Mary's *Songs, Threnody*, and *In the Beginning* (the first two sections of "Adam" and "Adam and Eve").[49]

To this point, the company had staged many performances at the theatre of the Riverside Church, but the neighborhood was changing and becoming questionable after dark. The company needed to find another location to perform. In June 1974, the company performed at the New York University Theater, which had been adapted to present concert dance. Mary premiered her new work *Chasm* to music by Karel Husa.

The idea to choreograph *Chasm* came to Mary as she observed the homeless, drug addicts, students, and people who had various mental disorders. Each day she walked among these people as she left her West 14th street apartment and walked to the East side to her studio at 736 Broadway. Later, Mary described *Chasm* for the films that she donated to the Film Archive of the Dance Collection of the New York Public Library for the Performing Arts. Mary said,

> Until I created Chasm, I had choreographed mostly dramatic or lyric works. With *Chasm* I wished to experiment and, using a contemporary score, create a work based on my experiences.
>
> *Chasm* deals with observations of the street of which I live on and with my work at the Women's House of Detention. It is about under-privileged teenagers who will kick an old woman to death for 70 cents, and about the paranoid fear of old women on the street. It is also about a young man who battles drug addiction and about a prostitute (like the beautiful girls on 8th Avenue) who temporarily gives

him hope. But in the end all these people are separated by the *Chasm* of our time.

My own criticism of the work is that although I was aware of the above elements, I was unable to incorporate into *Chasm* the humanity necessary to make the work totally moving.[50]

Doris Diether, dance critic for *Village Life*, wrote an article on June 20, 1974 for the New York University concert, and of the premiere of Mary's *Chasm* she quoted Mary: "It deals with the chasm between people and between the generations" and the evil and fear in the streets. But Mary Anthony was not pessimistic about the future. Diether wrote that Mary has faith in the young people of today, "…even though they don't have all the answers either." Diether observed, "The modern drug culture and the specters of estrangement and dissociation were evoked. It was powerfully conveyed by Muriel Cohan, with the collaboration of Gwendolyn Bye and the versatile Mr. Maloney." Reviewer Robert J Pierce of the *The Village Voice* wrote of the premiere work "The dance is very Sokolowian in its basic theme and movement, particularly in the use of emotional gesture."[51]

For this June concert series, Mary's company performed three of her older works consisting of *Threnody, Antiphon*, and the "Adam" portion of *In the Beginning*. The company also performed Sokolow's *Rooms*, Parkes' *Tides* and *1 2 3 4 5*, and Maloney's *Power*. Additionally, the company premiered two works by Maloney: *Renascent Visions* to the music Ralph Vaughn Williams, and *Four Glances* to music by Valerie Simpson, Dorothy Morrison, Gloria Spencer, and Edwin Hawkins Singers. *Four Glances* had four movements: Look Out, New Look, Look Forward, and Look Up. *Village Life* reviewer, Doris Diether wrote,

> The first was *Four Glances*, a frenzied but euphoric creation danced to a pre-recorded jazz-rock score. This brought on the two guests Beth Shorter and Carl Paris. The second was *Renascent Visions*, a half surrealist, half lyrical evocation in which both Maloney and Mary Anthony had prominent roles.

Of June 1974 concert series *Dance Magazine* critic Nancy Moore wrote, "Mary Anthony is reputed to be a fine modern dance instructor. The members of her company, most of whom were trained by her, are very attractive and confident performers." Moore also commented on Mary's premiere *Chasm*. She wrote, "*Chasm* seemed to describe the brutal destruction of a family and/or heterosexual love relationship by a group of modishly dressed teenagers."

Critic Don McDonagh from The New York *Times* wrote notably of Sokolow's *Rooms*. He said, "In all, the company gave *Rooms* a strong and haunting performance."[52]

Thanks to the Artists in the Schools Program, Mary's company enjoyed touring for residencies in which the company would teach classes and give demonstrations for periods spanning a few days to a couple of weeks, each of which culminated in performances. In some of the places they went, she would select three students to perform a small but important part alongside the company in *Threnody*. In 1975, the company went to Versailles Walnut Elementary School in McKeesport, Pennsylvania from January 6–17. Returning to New York for just a few days, they went to Kent State University from January 30 through February 1 before immediately leaving for Richmond, Kentucky to perform at Eastern Kentucky University from February 3–5. This was followed by a residency in St. Paul, Minnesota at Johnson and Central High School from February 6–20.

When they returned to New York, Mary began working on a new piece of choreography. She choreographed *Seascape* to music by La Montaine titled "Birds of Paradise." Over the years, Mary had spent as much time as she could near the ocean. She was inspired by the ocean itself and all of the life that is sustained by it. Later, in 1975, the company performed this new premiere from October 9–12 at Marymount Manhattan Theatre in New York. Additionally, the company performed some of their older works along with Daniel Maloney's premiere pieces titled *Minstrel Show* to music by Taj Mahal and *Night Bloom* to a music collage. Critic Jack Anderson from *Dance Magazine* wrote,

> The Mary Anthony Dance Theatre left no doubt about what sort of company Anthony is striving to build. Here is a passionate company dedicated to humanistic concerns, a company which seeks to express in dance both human folly and grandeur.

Of Mary's earlier work, *Gloria*, Anderson wrote,

> But I have a hunch that Anthony wanted her *Gloria* to be considerably more than an exercise in jumping for joy. With its motifs of arms crossed tightly across the body in pious introspection and then flung wide with exaltation, it seems to be trying to express spiritual rapture.

Of her new work *Seascape*, Anderson wrote, "The dancers' arms lightly beat the air or fluttered rapidly, and their bodies stretched upwards as though about to rise in flight."

After this premiere, the company went right back on tour to Brigham Young University on November 28, where they performed the new work

Seascape with *Gloria*, *Threnody*, and "Adam" from *In the Beginning*. They then caught a plane and flew to Hawaii, where they performed in various locations from November 20–28. The tour was coordinated by the University of Hawaii along with Brigham Young University in Hawaii, Leward Community College, University of Hawaii at Hilo–CECS, Maui Community College, County of Kauai, and Hawaii State Dance Council.

In March 1976, Mary's company went on tour to perform in St. Louis, Missouri, and in March 1977, the company went to Elizabethtown, Pennsylvania to teach and perform with the school district. In January 1978, Mary went to the University of Illinois at Champaign/Urbana to guest teach and to set *Songs* on the advanced students. After six weeks in Illinois, Mary and her company went straight to Grand Rapids, Michigan to teach and perform at public schools. At the end of the two weeks in Grand Rapids, the company performed on March 2.

In the fall 1978 Mary's company went to Lee County in Fort Myers, Florida for a two-week residency that culminated in a performance at the end on September 23. The Fort Myers *News-Press* released a press release for the concert. Kathleen Powell, staff writer, interviewed Mary during one of their rehearsals before the show. In relation to Mary's work *In the Beginning*, Mary told Powell, "If you read the Bible carefully, I think you will see that I have found the correct psychological point of view of this story." Mary goes on to say,

> I don't want people who see our concert to think that I am not deeply sensitive to the spiritual. I am. I feel my understanding of the biblical account is deeply spiritual. I see God as an injured parent. He is hurt because Adam and Eve disobey—but somehow he does not disapprove. If he had, he would have destroyed them out of the Garden of Eden. I feel God accepts their eating of the forbidden fruit, for he knows that by doing so they are accepting life with all its pain, its joys, its sorrows. They have chosen to mature, instead of remaining children forever.

News-Press Art critic Gale Bennett for Fort Myers, Florida wrote a review especially about Mary's new work *Seascape*: "At times animal-like, at times serpentine, often in the nervous manner of the insects, the various dancers acted and reacted to each other in a sort of cause-and-effect choreography that was totally convincing. And once again, choreography and music displayed a beautiful marriage."

As part of the Lee County residency, the Lee County School Board hired artist Gregory Biolchini to paint a pastel of two of Mary's company members, Evelyn Shepard and George White. The finished painting was given to Tom Walters, who was the administrative coordinator for Lee

County's participation in the Artists-in-Schools residency. This painting now hangs in the Florida State Capitol's Art Collection in Tallahassee, Florida. The painting was made possible by the National Endowment for the Arts.

New York has an annual dance festival in the summers at the Delacorte Theater in Central Park, and the Mary Anthony Dance Theatre performed *Threnody* on September 9 and 10, 1978 as part of the festival.

Appearing again at the Riverside Theatre, the Mary Anthony Dance Theatre was a part of the Riverside Dance Festival. They performed June 14-15, 1979. New York *Times'* reviewer Jennifer Dunning wrote, "Mary Anthony has been one of the most quietly influential of the New York modern-dance teachers…Her well balanced and polished program and fine dancers of the Mary Anthony Dance Theatre proved that those old-fashioned virtues of craftsmanship and professionalism can be a lot more vibrant than they sound."

Of Mary's new choreography *Seascape*, Dunning wrote,

> It begins with a solo for a sea-mother Gwendolyn Bye, moves seamlessly into a duet for two crablike creatures, danced by William Adair and Steve Rooks, and ends with a slow processional for eight and a hint of coming disaster. From the slow-circling whirls of the solo to the spikey limbs at the end, the dance flows along with the kind of attenuated stretch and crumple of underwater life and focused precision of good dance.[53]

Dance News critic Susan Reiter wrote, "Her new *Seascape* successfully evokes imagery of the ocean. Birds on the horizon and entwining crabs are suggested, and the choreography meshes intelligently with the music."[54]

In March 1980, the company toured to Birmingham, Alabama, performing at the University of Alabama. Returning to New York, from June 12–15, 1980 the company performed again in the Riverside Dance Festival. The company premiered two of Mary's new works: *Triptych* to music by Phillip Lambro and *Lady of the Sea* to music by Elliot Weiss based on a song by Judy Collins. A review appeared in the New York *Times* by Jennifer Dunning. Of one of her new works, Dunning wrote, "*Triptych* is as dark as its score by Philip Lambro. Angst floats free, stabbed at by the splayed arms and silent screams of the first section, with its stretching approaches and withdrawals for four dancers."[55]

In late July 1980, Mary Anthony travelled to Cornish College in Seattle, Washington for a workshop. She choreographed a new piece on the advanced students, which was performed on August 1, 1980. The piece created exclusively for the Cornish dancers was called *Ecclesiastes III*.

Completing their fall schedule, the company went to Rhode Island to perform on November 22, 1980 as part of the Cumberland Arts in Education. On December 3 the company went to Union, New Jersey to perform at Kean College. And finishing their season for 1980, the company performed *Gloria* and *Ceremony of Carols* at the Washington Square Methodist Church from December 22–24. Constance Romero wrote a beautiful description and review of *Gloria*. It appeared in *In Step*. He said, "The work is a call to arms in war based on the idea that God is on our side. She (Mary) has a gesture that she uses in the choreography." Romero goes on to write,

> One particular gesture stood out: fingers and feet spread far apart, one arm raised directly up from the shoulder and the other crossed exactly in front of the waist. This gesture, which seeped to emphasize both the agony suffered from wars irreparable damage as well as the patriotism inspired by defending one's freedom, became the focus for the dancers' pulsating and directed energies.[56]

In May 1982, the Mary Anthony Dance Theatre celebrated its 25th anniversary with performances at Mary Mount Manhattan College. Henry Geldzahlep, Commissioner of the New York City Department of Cultural Affairs, sent Mary a telegram that stated, "Congratulations on the Twentieth Fifth Anniversary of your company your artistry and dedication to dance have brightened the city and the world." This, indeed, was a great moment.

Sadly, in 1985 Ross Parkes left New York to teach in Taiwan. Mary suffered his loss. To replace the classes he had taught at the studio, she hired Bertram Ross, who had been a principal dancer with the Martha Graham Dance Company.

Adding to the magnitude of losing Parkes, Mary was fighting the New York City Loft Board. Her landlord was working furiously to raise her rent, and she had to hire a lawyer to fight. By 1985, she owed the lawyer $10,000, which meant her company would never be the same. She would not be able to hire seasoned choreographers for her dancers. Plus, she was losing all of the great dancers she had in the late 60s and 70s.

In 1970, when I joined the company, the only way that Mary's choreography was reset was by the dancers' memories. Often, a tremendous amount of effort and time went in to reconstructing the works. Mary couldn't always remember them, as she had moved on the other works of choreography. Video had not been invented yet. I came up with the idea of filming the rehearsals. (Dancers of today may not know the difference between videotaping and literally "filming" a performance, because recording is still called "filming," but at that point, filming involved cutting and splicing actual reels of film.) For Christmas in 1971, I had received a Rollei Super 8 film camera that used three-minute cassettes of black and white film with no sound. With Mary's choreography being between 25 and 30 minutes each, I had to change the three minute cassettes constantly as I filmed. During subsequent rehearsals, I would try to film the segments I had missed while changing cassettes. If I myself was dancing in the piece of choreography, I would have a friend come and film for me.

Once the film was developed by a photo shop, they were out on small reels. I purchased splicing equipment and a movie view editor so I would be able to see where to splice together not only the reels, but to insert the missing segments. It was quite a lengthy process. When I finished putting together a complete work together, I gave the films to Mary Anthony. The only downside to this method was that there was no sound, rehearsals were filmed instead of performances, and the developed 8 mm film moves at a faster pace than it was recorded. Later in September 1974, Mary donated the films to the Film Archive of the Dance Collection of the New York City Library. The works that I filmed, along with Mary Anthony's notes, are detailed below. At the top of the donated works the list says, "Filmed by Mary Price during rehearsals preceding December 26–30, 1971 performances at the Theatre of the Riverside Church in New York City."

- *Antiphon*
  Choreography: Mary Anthony
  Music: Louis Calabro ("Symphony for Strings")
  Costumes: Susan McPherson.
  Dancers: Ross Parkes, Daniel Maloney, Aaron Osborne, Yuriko Kimura, Mary Price, and Muriel Cohan.
  * The music was given to Miss Anthony by Mr. Calabro after he had seen a performance of *Threnody* at Bennington College.

- *Gloria*
  Choreography: Mary Anthony
  Music: Francis Poulenc ("Gloria in G Minor")
  Costumes: Christina Giannini
  Dancers: Ross Parkes, Daniel Maloney, Mel Jones, Aaron Osborne, Yuriko Kimura, Elisa Monte, Muriel Cohan, Tonia Shimin, and Mary Price.

- *The Pursued*
  Choreography: Joseph Gifford
  Music: Traditional
  Dancers: The Woman: Mary Anthony and The Man: Ross Parkes

- *Songs*
  Choreography: Mary Anthony
  Music: Claude Debussy (String Quartet #1)
  Costumes: Eileen Holding
  Dancers:
  I. Yuriko Kimura, Elisa Monte, and Gwendolyn Bye
  II. Ross Parkes, Daniel Maloney, and Aaron Osborne
  III. Tonia Shimin and Ensemble
  * The music used is the first three movements.

- *To José Clemente Orozco*
  (Excerpt from the suite—Dedications in Our Time)
  Original Choreography: Lester Horton
  Reconstructed by: James Truitte
  Music: Kenneth Klaus
  Dancers: The Woman: Tonia Shimin and The Man: Daniel Maloney

- *A Ceremony of Carols*
  Choreography: Mary Anthony
  Music: Benjamin Britten
  Set: Thomas Munn
  Costumes: Leor C Warner II

In the library's agreement regarding the donation, Mary Anthony is allowed to borrow them anytime as needed. Resetting choreography was so much easier with the films. In Tonia Shimin's documentary film *Mary Anthony: A Life in Modern Dance*, she used excerpts of Mary dancing in *The Pursued* from the rehearsals I had filmed. After I left the company, they had some 16 mm format films made, which the company also donated to the library.

A Dancer's Journey "It All Started With A Lie" 125

Mary Anthony with Ann Rosegarten

736 Broadway, 7th Floor, Mary Anthony Dance Studio, photo by Claudia Sara Lacena

"In the Beginning" (Adam), Ross Parkes, photo by Kenn Duncan

"In The Beginning" (Adam), Ross Parkes, photo by Kenn Duncan

A Dancer's Journey "It All Started With A Lie" 127

Mary Anthony in "Gloria"

"Gloria", left to right - Tonia Shimin, Elisa Monte, Mary Anthony, Muriel Cohen, and Mary Price

Mary Anthony in "Gloria", photo by V Sladdon

"Dedication to José Clemente Orozco", left to right - Daniel Maloney, Tonia Shimin, James Truitt, photo by Kenn Duncan

"Dedication to José Clemente Orozco", Tonia Shimin and Daniel Maloney, photo by Kenn Duncan

"In the Beginning" (Eve), Yuriko Kimura and Ross Parkes, photo by Kenn Duncan

"In the Beginning" (Eve), Yuriko Kimura and Ross Parkes, photo by Kenn Duncan

"In the Beginning" (Cain and Abel", left to right - Tonia Shimin, Daniel Maloney, Aaron Osborne, and Ross Parkes, photo by V Sladdon

A Dancer's Journey "It All Started With A Lie" 131

Poster for the December 20, 1970 performance

Mary Anthony backstage, photo by V Sladdon

Mary Anthony and Ross Parkes after a performance

"Ceremony of Carols", Yuriko Kimura, photo by V Sladdon

"Chasm", left to right - Elaine Anderson, Muriel Cohen, Daniel Maloney, and Gwendolyn Bye, photo by Lewis Brown

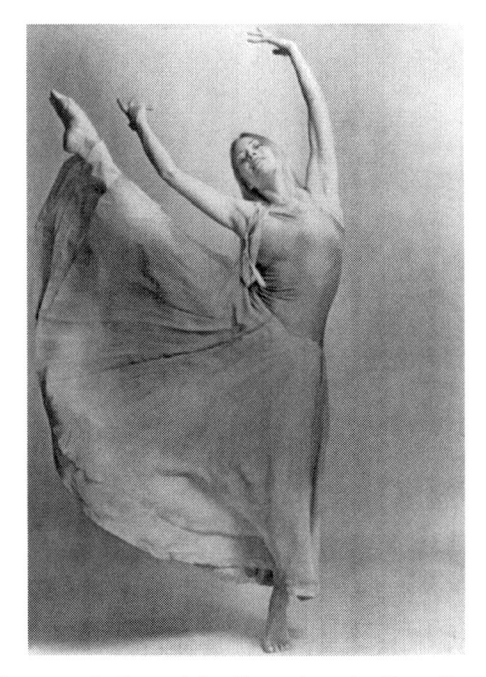

"Seascape", Gwendolyn Bye, photo by Kenn Duncan

Mary Anthony teaching at the University of Illinois, courtesy of the University of Illinois

Mary Anthony and William Warfield at the University of Illinois, courtesy of the University of Illinois

"Seascape", Mary Ford-Sussman, photo by Nan Melville

"Seascape", Mary Ford-Sussman, photo by Nan Melville

Pastel Painting by Gregory Biolchini of Evelyn Shepard and George White

CHAPTER 8

Mary's Philosophy

*I*n 1974 Tom Wetmore, one of Mary's students who was earning his Master of Fine Arts in dance from NYU, conducted seven interviews with Mary. During one of these interviews, Mary wanted to talk about the "things that make her down." She gets very upset "...when students—new students and the regular students—don't listen." Mary has reasons for each part of her well thought-out classes, which stem from the beautiful wonders of the world, art, opera, and humanity. For example, she will give dancers an inspiration such as "It is a beautiful day!" or "The bull fighter is entering the ring to fight the bull!" At the same time, Mary describes the technical requirement that the dancers need to incorporate as they dance. She often finds that "...young students don't respond with their faces and bodies, and they do the steps showing they didn't listen or they didn't care.

"Today many dance students are in a time where nobody looks, nobody listens, nobody smells. The air is polluted, and they don't taste their food," she said. "They seem to have lost all of their five senses." Mary marveled at the refined awareness of her grandmother, who could feel linen with her fingers and know if it was Hungarian or Irish.

One day around this time, Mary and a musician who helped shape modern dance, Louis Horst, had lunch together, and he had a similar complaint with his composition classes. Many years ago when Louis taught composition classes at the Martha Graham studio, every one of his 20 students would return with their assignment of choreography completed. But today, of the 20 students, only two or three complete their assignments.

Anna Sokolow complained of the very same thing when she taught composition classes. Anna told Mary, "Young people of today are very harassed and upset and kind of floundering around." Anna also felt they are not willing to make an artistic commitment. The students have numerous excuses of why they don't have time to listen to music, visit art museums, and read poetry. Anna and Mary could not understand why these young people were "unhappy instead of doing." Mary feels that the time making excuses is wasted time indeed. Rather than creating reasons for not completing something, it is far easier to fulfill commitments. Dance students don't realize that the world of art will go on forever. This has been proven throughout history from cave paintings to exquisite art and jewelry from Egypt. As Mary says, "We only have one time to live. Art will live—

not the subways, streets, and noise. Students seem empty and frustrated." All Mary wants them to know is that "…there is a richness that has nothing to do with earning a living. Art calls the artist." In the case of dance, Mary always says, "Dance finds you." And, whatever the art form, you cannot imagine doing anything else. Money is not part of the equation. Mary, herself is a living testimony to her philosophy. Yes, life has challenges, of all sizes, but Mary has persevered in keeping her dance studio alive and well.

Another observation Mary mentioned to Wetmore is what she calls "studio hopping." Unlike years ago, she feels that students will approach a teacher and ask for a critique of their work. Then, rather than working on the correction, they go to another teacher and hope this new teacher will say everything is all right. They go from class to class and still don't listen. In an attempt to be versatile, they never truly master any particular style. Instead, Mary feels that students should make a commitment to a style. They need to decide if they want Limon, Graham, Anthony, etc. They need to stay in that style long enough to know what the commitment is. If they want to rebel thereafter or change to another style, that is their privilege. Mary often mentions that Hanya used to say, "A single class should be like a shot in the arm that makes you go off and work by yourself." Mary's feeling is that "Dancers of today want the art given to them, rather than giving to the art. When you give to the art, then you are fed by the art."

It is so important to "reach these young people of today," Mary noted. Dancers are not born passive; they have learned this behavior by growing up in a passive society. During one of her teaching tours in 1977, an article in *The Salt Lake Tribune* summed up her distress. In the piece titled, "Trust your bodies, they're wiser than you think," Helen Forsberg wrote, "Miss Anthony strongly believes arts programs, particularly dance, are necessary for students of all ages." Underneath a photo of Mary appeared the caption "Dancer Mary Anthony believes today's teenagers are passive. She wants to get them back into enjoying activity." In the article Mary stated, "It's today's high school students who worry me. They're much more passive than they were ten years ago. They're either bused or driven to and from school. Then they go home and do homework and watch television. I want to get them back into enjoying activity."

Mary believes, too, that allowing children to watch so much television creates passiveness. She does credit television shows such as *Sesame Street* that educate children, but her disappointment with even these programs is their lack of physical activity. Because of television, children's involvement and imagination is missing. Mary said to Forsberg, "I think these young students want someone to shock them out of passivity. In our affluent society, the kids take the attitude of 'give me something'. But, way in the back I can see a glitter in their eyes. If we can touch one student deeply, then I feel it will be worth it."

When Mary and her company traveled to various schools to teach and perform, she could read the body language of young girls based on the way they carried their bodies as they walked down the school hallways. Lacking identity, they needed to be like famous people to feel a sense of security. Forsberg quoted Mary when she wrote, "In a dance class here at the high school, I have fifteen Farrah Fawcetts." Mary feels that children need to be taught that they are each unique. So often, she finds that fathers push their sons to be athletes. Mary found over the years that many young men who had been athletes later discovered that dance answered their calling. Because of the stigma against boys dancing, Mary never used the word "dance" during these school residencies. Instead, she used the word "movement." Again Forsberg quoted Mary, "What parents don't realize is that the discipline and accurateness that is learned through the movement classes is often carried over into other areas, such as mathematics class. Frequently I'll have a football or basketball coach sneak through the back door and ask me if I'll teach the athletes. The boys in my classes have reluctance at first, but they eventually get caught up in movement, and usually do the most work."

On another tour, Mary was aghast at how a teacher dismissed a student as "unteachable." The teacher told Mary not to pay any attention to one particular student who she characterized as "not very bright." Mary hates it when teachers give a young child a label and discount that student. Instead, Mary wants to believe in every student. That exact same labeled child excelled in Mary's classes, and Mary had the student lead the other students with success. Because she was only at this school for a couple of weeks, she hoped the teacher observed the potential that the student had and that this validated the student's inherent value both to the teacher and to the student.

Mary also feels the face is the most important muscle a dancer has in the theater. This is especially important when picking dancers for her company. In her interviews with Tom Wetmore, Mary told him that Gwendolyn Bye was a beautiful girl and dancer. She was bigger than other company dancers that she had hired over the years. In spite of her weight, however, she was an artist who spoke to the audience from the inside. "There is a big difference with dancers who technique their way through class and those who really dance beyond technique," Mary continued. "So, in other words, I don't care about the technique, I really don't. In the end, it is important that if you can't say something with it, it doesn't mean a thing…Great art has to have form, precision, and communication." Mary also looks for a kind of freedom in the body for her company dancers. "Unless you can identify with the inner line, the inner emotive line, the movement just becomes movement. I want each dancer in my company to be able to express through their bodies the line, the emotive line of the word we may be doing at the moment."

Mary's original company had three tiny girls and three very tall girls, and Mary choreographed for that combination. She loves to give the example of Balanchine, who choreographed for each of his dancers. The choreography that he gave Melissa Hayden and the choreography that he gave Violette Verdy was different. "A choreographer uses the bodies he or she happens to have at the moment and hopes that whatever ultimate bodies will replace them will be able to do what they do," she said. She gave the example of Anthony Tudor. He choreographed a dark and emotive role for Hugh Laing and Nora Kaye. Tudor choreographed for the particular people he had at the time he was working with them. For example, when Mary choreographed the second part, "Eve," of *In the Beginning*, she made it especially for Ross Parkes and Yuriko Kimura. She found herself being very creative because the two dancers are "...emotive, and their bodies not only work well together, they are magical." When Mary choreographed the first part, "Adam," she was struck by a poem of what it must have meant to Adam as the sun went down for the very first time. He didn't know that there would be another day. Mary created "Eve" in the summer when Mary didn't have a performance deadline. Also, Yuriko and Ross were free and wanted to work. Mary remembers they came to the studio laughing and having fun, and Mary said "We're going to start." And they said "Yes." And Mary said "Would you lie down." They knew Mary was ready to work, and they were "marvelous to work with". Furthermore, they were willing to work the whole summer. And for Mary, it was a "most creative time." Creating this second part of *In the Beginning*, "Eve," was like the time when she created *Threnody* at Bennington, where the dancers were willing to try anything. If something didn't "work out," they were willing to "work it out." When the "Eve" section was finally complete, Yuriko and Ross came over and sat in Mary's lap and said "This is it! This is it!" Yuriko and Ross were "deep, emotive dancers." They were technically good, but they worked beyond that. And, Mary said that for each movement, they wanted to know the story behind the movements they were dancing. So many other dancers just want the steps.[57]

Mary feels there are two paths in modern dance: dancing for technique or using the technique to tell a story. Of the two approaches, she felt that very few put the human element into the dance. Too many dancers are only interested in technique. Again, this goes back to the student hopping from studio to studio to studio, taking a lot of technique classes, but not getting involved emotionally. Mary said, "It is like when you attend dance [concerts] and you are only watching the design, and not being caught up emotionally."

The advice that Mary gives young aspiring dancers who want to dance professionally or become choreographers is that they must make the time commitment consistently to the craft of dance technique, workshops, and so forth. She feels that today's dancers are scattered. They think they want to be dancers, but they will use earning a living as an excuse for the lack of time commitment. Mary says that you have to make the time.

While she insists that money must not be the goal of art, Mary has become discouraged occasionally over the years with financial problems. Many times, when her studio doesn't get enough revenue for her to pay herself, she choreographs and teaches for free, and she is only able to survive through guest artist bookings. Her dedication to her art form is consummate.

In his 1980 article, "The Mary Anthony Approach," Jack Anderson wrote, "Like many choreographers and company directors, Miss Anthony has her troubles. There is never enough money and she is in great need of a company manager. Yet she continues and continues happily, 'I like to think we're a sort of family in our studio', she said. Referring to her co-directors, Mr. Maloney and Mr. Parkes, she noted, 'We've been working together for fourteen years now. That alone suggests that things are going right for us.'"

No doubt, Mary has had many ups and downs. By 1983, the prior 15 years had been absolute glory, especially after coming from such humble beginnings. She was now on the threshold of two big changes. By 1983, the major members of the Mary Anthony Dance Theatre had left to pursue their own teaching and choreography. She understood because she too had taken flight from Hanya. Mary was heartbroken, and yet she still wanted to create and work. She formed another company that she called Phoenix, which means rising from the ashes. The mission statement of Phoenix states,

> A developing modern dance repertory company, Phoenix represents the new Mary Anthony Dance Theatre—an offspring of the internationally acclaimed Mary Anthony Dance Theatre which celebrated its twentieth fifth anniversary in 1982. After three years of regrouping and revitalizing, Phoenix directs its focus on dance in the 1980's with a unique approach. Beyond maintaining and reconstructing important classical modern dance pieces by noted choreographers—Charles Weidman, Anna Sokolow, Lester Horton, Mary Anthony, Daniel Maloney, and William Adair, Phoenix fosters the development of new works by its own company members under the guidance of artistic director Mary Anthony.

Showing guts and courage, Mary forged ahead and did very well. Beyond maintaining and reconstructing important classical modern dance pieces by noted choreographers Charles Weidman, Anna Sokolow, Lester

Horton, Daniel Maloney, and William Adair, Phoenix developed new works by its own company members under Mary's guidance as artistic director, and Mary continued to create new works for this new company. Whenever dancers from her previous company performed, she called them guest artists ("former soloists with the original Mary Anthony Dance Company").

In the spring of 1985, Phoenix gave performances in smaller venues before their New York debut by participating in SAGE (Service to the Aging) with six performances that were free to the public. They also performed for a 6th grade class in New York and had a showing with Ron Brown on June 6–7 with selected company members.

Phoenix's real debut program was June 17, 1985 at the Dance Theatre Workshop Showing and consisted of a new work by Mary called *In Celebration of W.P. Yeats* to music by James Galway and George Winston. She presented this piece with the following comment: "In Memory of The Red Rose, The White Birds, and Coole Park, 1929." Also performed were *7:45 AM* choreographed by William Adair, *The Courtship of Arthur and Al* choreographed by Charles Weidman, *The Waltz* choreographed by Susan Jacobson, and Mary's older works *Songs* and *Antiphon*. Following the performances of newly created Phoenix, critic Jennifer Dunning of the the New York *Times* wrote,[58]

> Dance doesn't seem to take much stock of its wise elders. Among those veterans is Mary Anthony, one of the city's most highly respected modern dance teachers. And a performance by the new Mary Anthony Dance Theatre/Phoenix on Wednesday at the Theater of the Riverside Church on Claremont Avenue and 120th Street suggested that Miss Anthony still has much to tell us after 42 years in dance, and one of the messages of the program is that well-trained dancers can be encouraged to move expressively in a way that gives full value to each moment on the stage. That quality brought an extra eloquence to Miss Anthony's lyrical *Songs* (1956). The group work is set to Debussy's searing String Quartet, played here by the Algonquin String Quartet, and looks to Miss Anthony's memories of being young and in love in Paris...*Songs* evokes that time of joyful, slightly sad suspension between childhood and adult responsibility. The dance's final, lovely moments—when the dancers rock softly in sedate pairs, stepping forward and back as if marking points on a compass—suggests the expectation of companionable courtship...The sensitive performers were Susan Jacobson, Patricia Auwapara, Erin Morrell, Heidi Putman, Ron Brown, John Guidice, and Shahab Nahvi.

Doris Diether also gave a wonderful review for Mary's new company in *The Villager* on June 27, 1985 titled "Downtown: New Company Worth Watching." In her article, Diether said,

For their introductory concert at the Bessie Schoenberg Theater, this young, lively group performed a varied program...Like Anthony's former company, this new group is well trained and, although each of the dancers has a definite personality, they can also dance well in ensemble works. This looks like a company to watch.

In the fall of 1985 they performed as part of the 4th Annual Downtown Dance Festival Series in lower Manhattan, and they also participated in Riverside Dance Festival Performance Series from December 4–8.

Mary's second huge change would be twofold: rent was rising, and she would soon lose her apartment and maybe even her studio.

Phoenix, from left to right - Kristie Egtvedt and front right is Linda Hayes, photo by Jay Crane

CHAPTER 9

Greedy Landlord and Forging Ahead

By 1983, the area where Mary's studio is located was transitioning from an inexpensive artists' neighborhood to a trendy, expensive locale, and her landlord wanted to raise her rent excessively. This often happens in large cities, particularly where artists find places to rent that they can afford. Artists will move to these locations, and within just a few years, the artists have attracted interest in the neighborhood. Developers see this interest and start fixing up the neighborhood. Before you know it, the artists cannot afford to live there anymore and are forced to move as their rents increase.

In 1969 when Mary first rented her loft space at 736 Broadway, it was not a very good neighborhood, which made the rent affordable. During those years, she kept a separate apartment in the West Village, but in 1983, she moved into her studio, hoping to avoid a rent increase by the "loft law" that applied to residential leases. The loft law only protected tenants who lived in their loft; not if they were using the loft for a commercial business. This applied to multiple-dwellings in New York and it applied to people in approximately 1,000 commercial buildings in New York City. Unfortunately for Mary, the same year she moved into her studio, the city Loft Board ruled that a loft space was residential only when one could prove that one was living in the loft between 1980 and 1981 for at total of at least 16 months. The board decided that Mary's space was commercial rather than residential. This meant that the residential rent-stabilization rules did not apply and that her landlord could charge whatever he wanted. Mary did not give up. She told the loft board that students had been living there from 1969 through 1983 when she had moved in.

Friends and students rallied to support her, writing letters to Mayor Koch. Liz Aaronson, a former student living in Williamsburg, Massachusetts, wrote,

> A 71-year-old artist is under threat of eviction from her home/studio loft of almost twenty years, threatened by a landlord who has decided that a business-for-profit in that space would bring him much more income than he's now enjoying. Because this artist lives, as she always has, on the small income she receives by teaching, she cannot afford the vastly increased rent, as he knew she could not.

Speaking of Mary's studio, Liz says, "Mary creates, as only great teachers do, a safe place to fumble, get it wrong, need to see the combination again, ask questions; and then, space to create, perform, collaborate, teach…Her students, and former students, ask not that you pity, but that you cherish this woman, and that by vigorously and personally affirm what is great about New York."

Mayor Koch received letters from hundreds of dancers, teachers, and friends that Mary has influenced over her lifetime—among them mine—as well as Patricia Knowles, dance chair at the University of Illinois. Mayor Koch responded to each and every one letter, and the story even reached the New York *Times*. On January 12, 1988 an article appeared in *Times* titled "Dancer Is Facing Loss of Studio in New York." Sarah Lyall wrote,

> Mary Anthony, a renowned teacher and choreographer of modern dance, is facing imminent eviction from the lower Manhattan studio where she has worked for 20 years, and she says she is the victim of a vindictive landlord and an unfair city ruling. Yesterday, about 80 dancers, friends and students of Miss Anthony gathered at City Hall to protest her plight. Now 71 years old, she has taught many of New York's most important modern dancers at her studio at 736 Broadway, between Astor and Waverly Places, which now doubles as her home. If she is evicted, Miss Anthony said, she does not know where she will go or what will happen to her school. Miss Anthony's former students include Donald McKayle, the choreographer, Arthur Mitchell, director of Dance Theater of Harlem, and a member of Martha Graham's Dance Company, including Jacquelyn Buglisi and George White, Jr.…'There should be some kind of protection for people of her caliber', said Bertram Ross, who was a leading dancer in the Graham Company and now teaches at the Mary Anthony Dance Studio. "It's not like someone who's just starting in; this is a woman who's paid her dues.

Lyall talked with the loft board director Lee Fawkes, and he explained, "The hearing officer gave an objective reading and full and careful consideration of the facts. He found the loft was not used for residential purposes under the statute, that it was a dance studio and not a residence." Fawkes told Lyall, "It was a hard case for us, and we're not happy to see a 70-year-old woman put out onto the streets in the middle of winter. But, it is the board's job to apply the statute and to look at the facts."[59]

Mary appealed in court. Other tenants were in the same predicament and were fighting against the landlord, William Muschel. Lyall said,

> In 1985, the city appointed an administrator to collect rent and make repairs in the building after tenants complained about poor maintenance by Mr. Muschel. Jane Mark, the administrator and a member of

the tenants' group, issued a lease to Miss Anthony, saying if the courts upheld the board's decision, she could keep her loft and pay $1,600 a month in rent. Miss Anthony had been paying $600 a month. Eviction Proceedings Began. The ruling was, in fact, upheld, and Miss Anthony began paying the rent last summer. But Mr. Muschel went to court, arguing that the administrator lacked the power to issue such a lease. The lease was declared invalid, and Miss Anthony received an eviction notice in December.

Mary appealed the lease and her eviction. Unfortunately her hearing wasn't scheduled until January 20, 1988, a month after her eviction. Mr. Muschel, her landlord, told her she could stay without a lease for $2,500 per month—money that Mary Anthony did not have. Mary's lawyer appealed for a stay of eviction until her case could be heard. In her article, Lyall continued, "The tenants say that Mr. Muschel resents them for forming a tenants' association and that he is singling out Miss Anthony because she is not protected by the loft law."

Administrator Mark said, "It's total meanness on his part." The administrator knew the landlord before she was appointed, and she said, "The landlord had a history of failing to provide basic services, like heat, electricity, and water."

On January 23, 1988, another article appeared in The New York *Times* titled "Dance Teacher Wins Stay of Eviction Order." The article said, "Mary Anthony, the modern dance teacher who was to be evicted from her loft in lower Manhattan this week, was granted a stay of the eviction order yesterday after the Loft Board said it would consider reopening her case." Mary was granted the stay of the eviction order from her lawyer's appeals and all of the letters that went to Mayor Koch. In the end, Mary's loft was considered a commercial space, and after all of this grief, she ended up paying $2,000 per month ($1,400 more than she had paid previously). Furthermore, she owed her lawyer $80,000. As a result, she was able to keep her space, but she could no longer afford to bring in other choreographers, buy new costumes, and so forth. But, she persevered continuing to teach and sometimes have the company perform. She also began to give small, intimate concerts in her studio. Mary taught the students her choreography, and two to three times a year they would have an in-studio performance. Occasionally, another organization would host them, and they would perform in a theater.

On June 11, 1993 The American Dance Guild presented The New Dance Group Gala Concert, a historic retrospective of the New Dance Group, from the 1930s through the 1970s, and Mary Anthony was listed on the cover of the program. Indeed, she was one of the dancers instrumental in the early years (the 40s and early 50s) of the New Dance Group. Ruth W. Messinger, City of New York Borough President wrote a letter celebrating The New Dance Group project. The gala was co-sponsored by the Dance Department of the LaGuardia High School of the Performing Arts.

At this gala performance Mary presented a section from her choreography of *Songs* (1956): Part III, "To Each His Own." The dancers were Gia T Cacalano, Pamela Dent, Mary Ford, John S. Guidice, John Passafiume, Jon T. De Vries, and Warner Williams. On June 15, 1993, Jennifer Dunning reviewed the performance for the New York *Times* writing, "From the opening number, a hauntingly lyrical excerpt from Mary Anthony's 1956 *Songs*... the emphasis was on simplicity and an ageless craft."

On December 6 and 7, 1996, Mary Anthony Dance Theatre had it 40th Anniversary Celebration at the Sylvia and Danny Kaye Playhouse at Hunter College. These two performances were very special in that many previous company members and students attended. The lobby of the theater was adorned with photos and posters of Mary's 40 years of work. For this performance she integrated *Phoenix* dancers with members of the original company calling the company by its former name. Her dancers were Mary Ford, Kun-uang-Lin, Pamela Luedtke, Kori Darling, Daniel Charon, Ru-Ping Want, Renee D'Aoust, Adam Klotz, Sandra Antognazzi, Andre Megerdichian, Chiung-Wei Teeng, Juan Carlos Gonzales, Ariane Anthony, Valerie Szurdak, and Emma Hogarth, with special guest artists Gwendolyn Bye and Daniel Maloney. Ross Parkes was her rehearsal director. The program consisted of Mary's premiere of *Tabula Rosa*, along with *Ceremony of Carols, In the Beginning* (Part 3, "Cain and Abel"), *Songs*, and *Threnody*. The music for *Tabula Rosa* is Arvo Part, and Mary uses a quote from Euripides in the program, which says, "For who knows if the thing that we call death is our life and our life dying. Who can know?"

Jennifer Dunning wrote a review in the New York *Times* titled "From Anguish Onward, a Course in Emotions." In her review, she gave much due respect to Mary Anthony and her longevity and quality of her work. Dunning was taken by the "intensity of the emotions" of Mary's choreography and the performance of the dancers. Dunning wrote, "Ms. Anthony, who turned 80 this year, has been around long enough and done enough on modern dance and Broadway stages to be able to step back and take a long look at her subject matter."

Of the new premiere, Dunning wrote, "*Tabula Rosa* is at heart a stark, formal juxtaposition of two dancers with each other and a group." She commented on the Euripides quote saying, "There is no clear reference to this, performers seem swept along by the force of an anguish devastating in its impersonality." In the piece, the two lead dancers remain together as a couple throughout the work with the corps either circling them or passing them on a diagonal path. Dunning goes on to write, "Ms Anthony has caught just the right balance between individual and group, vivid detail and grand overarching theme."

Another review appeared in *Dance Magazine* written by Muriel Topaz. Of *Tabula Rosa*, Topaz wrote, "The premiere shows the continuing creativity of this remarkable woman." Of Mary's older classic work, Topaz wrote, "*Songs* is, quite simply, a glorious display of impassioned dancing; I cannot imagine why the work has not been snatched by repertory companies across the country." Of the entire concert, Dunning wrote "Anthony's choreographic strengths lie in the clarity of exposition of her ideas, the clean, secure structures of all of the dances, and, most of all her extraordinary musical sensitivity."

In addition to holding performances in her own studio, another inexpensive place Mary and her company could perform in was the Cunningham Studios. The Merce Cunningham facility held a space in which small companies could perform. The Merce Cunningham Foundation closed in 2012; thus, this space is no longer available. Mary's company was able to enjoy it during its time, however. Gus Solomons, Jr. wrote an article titled "Against the Odds, They Keep on Making Dance" that was published in the New York *Times* on February 11, 2001. Solomons wrote, "Everyone who's aware of dance has heard how grueling it is, how intrepid dancers brave financial hardship, physical pain and lack of proper respect to pursue their passions." He bemoans that concert dance is being pushed aside by big business. Solomons noted six dance artists with age ranges of 63 to 84, with Mary being the oldest. Observing Mary teach, he was amazed that this lady at 84 was demonstrating the steps as she taught her class. He adored her famous class imagery. Quoting Mary Anthony, he said, "Imagine you're wearing big red boots! Now add four Chagall poses at the end. You all know Chagall's paintings?"

In the beginning of the 21st century, Mary Anthony made a comeback with her company. In December 2001, the company performed at the theater of the Riverside Church. A dancer named Kun-Yang Lin assisted Mary in the endeavor. Jennifer Dunning wrote a review of the program in the New York *Times* on December 18, 2001 titled, "Dance In Review; Do Whatever With It, It's Still Modern Dance." Dunning wrote, "Mary Anthony has trained several generations of dancers and choreographers over her 45 year career. One of the gifts she has given them is a sense of bedrock modern dance to use or depart from." From 1971, Mary's *A Ceremony of Carols*, set to the Benjamin Britten score, opened with the scene of the "Angel of the Annunciation," which had been originally set on Yuriko Kimura. The solo was danced by company member Ruping Wang. Dunning wrote, "[Wang] made every subtle dynamic change and position clear in this little gem, so delicate at times that it seemed a mere flick of a white-robed body." Mary even set her *In the Beginning* on Chi-Tsung Kuo, as Adam and Ruping Wang, as Eve. Of the two Dunning wrote,

> Chi-Tsung Kuo was a lithe young Adam, full of poignant doubt and optimism as he learned to move upright and was drawn to a mysterious tree. Ms. Wang was his snakelike Eve. Intriguingly, the 1969 duet, set to shimmering music by Peter Sculpthorpe suggests that the first man and woman had traces in them of the animals that preceded them. As intriguing are the glints of Asian influence in the music and choreography, at least as performed by these two Taiwanese dancers.

Originally, the dancers were Ross Parkes from Australia and Yuriko Kimura from Japan.

The New York Dance and Performance Awards (also known as the Bessies) have several categories of awards. In 2003–2004 Mary received the "Special Citation Award" naming her a "Dedicated Teacher and Mentor" and saying, "For fierce and unquenchable devotion as a revered teacher, choreographer, and cherished icon of modern dance; for decades of gracing New York with an elegant presence, armed with a love of the field and the sheer will to survive within it, resilient, beautiful and seemingly immortal." The program included quotes of outstanding reviews from *Threnody* and *Songs*.

One of the many things Mary has done is to be an adjudicator for the American College Dance Festival. In 2005, the American College Dance Festival gave tribute to the dancers and choreographers who have adjudicated for them, and Mary was among those honored.

CHAPTER 10

Mary's Cats

Cats have held a special place in Mary's heart since she was introduced to them not long after she opened her 61-4th Avenue studio. A friend of Mary's wanted to give her a studio-warming present, and this required Mary to accompany her to Queens, New York. The two made a day of it. At her friend's apartment, they first had a bite to eat complimented by martinis. Her friend then announced, "Now it is time!" She opened the door to the attic, and Mary only took one step up when a small, cuddly Siamese kitten ran up to her and scurried underneath her skirt. Mary's friend explained, "The kitten has chosen you, Mary." This started Mary's great love of cats.

Mary immediately gave her new furry kitten the name Alexandra. Anywhere Mary went, the cat was sure to go. They traveled on the plane to Italy, starting the flight with Alexandra in a small box under Mary's seat. The plane wasn't completely full with passengers, so Mary brought Alexandra out of her box, and everyone on the plane fell in love with her new cat, including the pilot. Alexandra got right into his lap.

When Mary was working in Italy, Alexandra attended all of the rehearsals. When she needed to relieve herself, she would make a small sound that Mary recognized. Excusing herself for a few minutes, Mary would take the cat to the ladies room, where Mary had a little pan set aside. After her pet finished her business, they both returned to the rehearsal.

Alexandra even climbed the Pyramids with Mary. She went to Mexico and watched Mary teach. Alexandra was a very bright cat, and she lived to the ripe old age of 18 years. But for humans, this is not very long. Mary couldn't stand it when the life of her beloved friend was taken.

During Alexandra's life, Mary decided her cat needed to "get married" as Mary puts it. A friend of Mary's had a male Siamese cat, who became the father of Alexandra's first six beautiful, blue-eyed Siamese kittens. Mary kept three of the kittens—two girls and one boy—and she gave the other three kittens away to friends. The names for her new babies were Anastasia, Holly, and Butch Cassidy.

Cats became a huge presence in Mary's life and in the birth of her dance studio. It wasn't long before her kitten Holly became pregnant, and she gave birth to six kittens just like her mother. After Alexandra passed away, Mary gave Butch Cassidy to Daniel Maloney. He lived at the time, and still lives, in the loft on the floor below Mary. Mary would take Holly and Anastasia with her on trips just as she had done with Alexandra. The two cats escorted her on the train and the ferry when she went to Fire Island to rejuvenate in a quiet retreat with the sound of the ocean waves.

Holly lived to 17 years when her health began to fail, and Mary had to make the difficult decision to put her to sleep. After Mary lost both Holly and Anastasia, she didn't want any more Siamese cats. She became so attached to them that her heart broke when they died.

A friend from the studio, Joe Meso, left Mary a note saying he knew she didn't want any more cats, but he had a friend with kittens that needed a home. Mary accompanied Joe to see the kittens, which were in a bundle ball on a bed. The ball broke up, however, as one kitten saw Mary and went marching up to her. Mary named her Felina. Felina was very small with a sad face. The woman who had the kittens convinced Mary she needed a second kitten so that Felina wouldn't get lonely. Selecting a boy, she first thought to name him Felino for Italian male. Instead, she named him Joey after her friend Joe.

Felina and Joey's younger days were spent climbing, running, chasing, fetching, and playing. In fact, Joey loved to climb a curtain that was used as a studio divider between the studio and the lounge area. This curtain was hung from the high ceiling and was directly next to the piano. Joey would run up the curtain and jump down onto the piano with a loud sound. When these cats were young, Mary had no mice. Mary was partial to Felina, because she felt that the animal was vulnerable. Joey, on the other hand, was very macho and could take care of himself.

As the two cats grew older, they followed Mary everywhere she went. When she sat down, they immediately got into her lap. When Mary left her studio to go shopping, some of the students would remain in the studio doing their scholarship duties such as watering the plants and vacuuming. They noted that as Mary emerged from the elevator, the cats knew that it was Mary. They would jump up on the desk right by to door to greet Mary when she entered.

Sadly Felina and Joey both grew old and died. As before, Mary was heartbroken. Finally, she decided to go to the animal shelter and get a grown cat, not a Siamese. The shelter, however, wouldn't let her adopt a cat, because they felt Mary was too old; she was only 93 years then. Depressed, she spoke to her veterinarian, who had the perfect solution. He gave Mary a grown cat that she named Tyger. Tyger follows her everywhere and gives her so much joy.

Mary Anthony with her kitten Alexandra

Alexandra at 1 year

Tyger

CHAPTER 11

Fire Island

During the seventies, Mary discovered Fire Island through Daniel and Ross, who went there often during the summers. It provided a refuge for the dancer Yuriko during a particularly difficult time. Yuriko Kimura is a beautiful person and was a gorgeous, sensitive dancer. Not only was she in the Martha Graham Company, but she was also in Mary's company. I remember the first time I saw her. It was after I had been accepted into Mary's company, and we were taking the advanced class from Mary. Yuriko's expression, her line, was something that I had never seen. When she lifted her leg, it spoke volumes. It was as if she stretched it reaching to the angels on high.

Richard Gain and Richard Kuch had been dating for a very long time. Both of them were soloists in the Martha Graham Company plus several Broadway musicals. Richard Gain was a soloist in Jerome Robbins Ballet USA. In 1971 or 1972, I danced in their company called Gaku. Still dancing for Mary, I also danced in Pearl Lang's Dance Company and Larry Richardson's Dance Company. All these companies were what I call "pick up," which means you are paid by the performance, not the weeks of rehearsal. Dancing with several companies at the same time was imperative to survive financially in New York.

The two Richards knew Yuriko and had worked with her in the Martha Graham Dance Company. Plus, they rented Mary's studio for their rehearsals. During this time, Yuriko and Richard Kuch became very close and were married. At one point, Richard left Yuriko, however. Devastated, Yuriko fell into a severe depression. Mary had Yuriko come to her 14th Street Apartment where she, Ross, and Daniel could keep an eye on her. Daniel worked at a hospital in New York City, and he knew a psychiatrist who agreed to come to Mary's apartment to see Yuriko.

Ross and Daniel also had a little place on Fire Island in an area called Cherry Grove. They felt that Yuriko needed to get out of the city and asked the psychiatrist if he thought that would be a good idea. He did indeed, except he said that Yuriko needed to be watched and cared for 24 hours a day. Because Daniel needed to stay in the city because of his work at the hospital, Mary, Ross, and Patrick Suzeau took Yuriko to Fire Island. With their constant care, Yuriko was able to return to her old self.

During this period with Ross and Daniel, Mary fell in love with Fire Island. It is right on the ocean, and it is beautiful. Mary felt that all her cares and worries from the studio and company were taken away with the waves of the sea. Ross told Mary about an area on the island called Fire Island Pines. In fact, Darrell Barnett and Lee Minskoff already had a place in the Pines. Darrell was a dancer I had the honor of training and taking to New York. He danced in Mary's company plus many companies in New York, the last of which was the Joffrey Ballet.

Mary wanted to come to the Pines on weekends during the summer months. Subsequently, she found a real estate agent named Arden Catlin, to whom she explained that all she needed was a little tiny place with a bed and a shower. Arden's first response was that she didn't have anything that fit that description. Leaving Mary alone for a bit, she returned to ask if she was serious in her request. Mary explained she was a dancer, and she just wanted a tiny retreat for the summer months. To Mary's delight, Arden said she had a guest house on her property. Together, they walked and Mary learned that the house at the top of the hill was where Martha Graham stayed. Walking and talking, Arden discovered that she liked Mary very much, and by the time they reached the guest house, it was a done deal—Mary could rent. Arden had a previous renter who made a lot of noise. Mary assured her she would be quiet. Mary paid Arden $1,000 in cash for the whole summer, which was a great bargain. Most places were $1,000 a day! The guest house was furnished, and Arden was so intent that Mary would never entertain, that she provided only one plate, one fork, and one spoon.

One summer I accompanied Mary and her cats from the city via train and ferry to Fire Island. It was a paradise. Mary told me she couldn't have anyone over to her guest house, but she did let me see her darling little abode. I stayed with Darrell, and Mary would come over for our interviews for this book. Darrell had danced in Mary's company before joining the Harkness Ballet and later the Joffrey Ballet. His place was within walking distance.

As Mary got to know Arden, she realized how much Arden loved nature. She knew every bird on the island, and she was an animal lover, too. She had six dogs. Arden's husband, Charlie, was an alcoholic, and Mary remembers one night hearing loud crashes coming from Arden and Charlie's house. She was frightened for Arden when Charlie was there with her. During the winter months, however, Charlie stayed on Fire Island, and Arden travelled to Florida. Charlie's drinking got the best of him and shortened his life.

After Charlie's death, Arden became friends with a man named Emerick Bronson. Arden had given him a standing invitation to come and stay at Fire Island, and Emerick accepted her invitation. When he visited, Arden and he had much fun together; Emerick would even bake Arden fresh, hot bread. He had made his living in photography, and he was well traveled. His witty humor cheered Arden.

There were also big parties on the island, which Arden and Emerick attended. Many of the parties had a theme—for example, one had an Egyptian theme. Both Arden and Emerick had a great time planning their costumes. Mary would provide her input.

There came a point at which Emerick and Arden were such close friends that they wanted to marry. The only problem was that because he was part of the gay community, he was worried some might think of him as a gold digger. First, Arden asked Mary what she thought about the marriage. Mary asked Arden some questions:

"Do you enjoy being together?"

Arden replied, "Yes, in fact, we stay up talking and laughing until 2AM every night."

Mary then gave her opinion. "People will talk no matter what, so do what will work for you and what will make you happy."

On one occasion Emerick drove Mary back into the city, and he asked Mary the same questions. Mary gave him the same answer. Emerick and Arden were eventually married. Thereafter, Emerick wanted to get a separate place for the two of them, but not on Fire Island. He felt that Fire Island was really Charlie's. Instead, they bought a place together in Sag Harbor. Now they had a place that was just theirs, Arden's and Emerick's.

While living on Sag Harbor, Arden began having heart problems. Even when Mary visited them, Arden would be too sick to join them for dinner. Not long after, Emerick called Mary with the sad news that Arden had passed away. Mary offered to visit him and keep him company, and he agreed. In time, the two became very close friends, but nothing romantic.

Mary was still able to go to Fire Island a bit longer, because Emerick had inherited Arden's property. He actually hated Fire Island. He didn't like the fact that it had been Charlie's; he didn't like sand; he didn't like heat; and he didn't like the community. Walter, a friend of Emerick's, encouraged him to sell the Fire Island property. It saddened Mary, but he did indeed sell it. Maia Helles, who had been a friend of Arden's, Emerick's, and Mary's on Fire Island was very upset that Emerick sold Arden's place. Maia invited Mary to her place on Fire Island, so Mary still had a place to get away. Maia and Mary became very close friends. Having a lot in common, they enjoyed dinners, English comedies, and movies. Maia was a ballerina in the Ballet Russes, and she is still in great shape, as she does her mother's Swedish exercises each and every day. In addition, she has a place in the city, where Mary also visits. To this day, Mary enjoys their special friendship.

In 2006, Mary was bestowed a Martha Hill Award, a very prestigious award for her significant contributions to dance. The Martha Hill Award is presented annually for demonstrated leadership in dance. The Martha Hill website includes the following quote,

> The Martha Hill Dance Fund was established to honor, perpetuate, and reward Martha Hill's commitment to dance education and performance internationally. As an educator, administrator, artistic director, and visionary for dance as a performing art, Martha Hill established an unprecedented standard for excellence in the field.[60]

Today, in 2012, Mary Anthony is still teaching an active schedule. She is 96 years old.

Mary Anthony and Mary Price Boday at the Martha Hill Awards

Mary Anthony and Joseph Gifford at her 95th Birthday 2011

Mary Price Boday and Mary Anthony at her 95th Birthday 2011

CHAPTER 12

Letters to Mary

*E*ach dancer, student, and friend who has known and worked with Mary has his or her own story. I wanted to make such stories part of this book. When Tom Wetmore interviewed Mary, she told him of a big envelope called "Reassurance." It contained the letters and notes from students and dancers who have worked with Mary. It was only after they each left Mary that they realized what Mary had taught them, and they have written thank you letters and letters of appreciation. Mary always says, "Unless we all think positively and do a positive thing each and every day, there isn't any hope."

The letters in this section are presented in alphabetical order:

1. Agresta-Stratton, Abigail
2. Blizzard, Mary Ellen
3. Boday, Mary Price
4. Bookspan, Audrey G.
5. Cohan, Muriel
6. Cox, Anne
7. Culley, Jane
8. Eshkenazi, Joan
9. Gallant, Catherine
10. Gilchrist, Rebecca
11. Gottschild, Brenda Dixon
12. Hansson, Eva
13. Hayes, Linda (Harris)
14. Jinks, Virginia Nill
15. Jowitt, Deborah
16. Knowles, Pat
17. Lowenstein, Lois
18. Lyn, Janaea Rose
19. Maloney, Daniel
20. Mauldin, Deborah
21. McKinley, Ann
22. Mitchell, Helen
23. Pastorella, Andrea
24. Phillips, Barbara Anne (Burns)
25. Rosen, Bernie
26. Shepard, Evelyn
27. Shimin, Tonia
28. Smith, Reuel
29. Stone, John
30. Suzeau, Patrick
31. Timm, Fred
32. Wetmore, Tom
33. Zema, Leslie

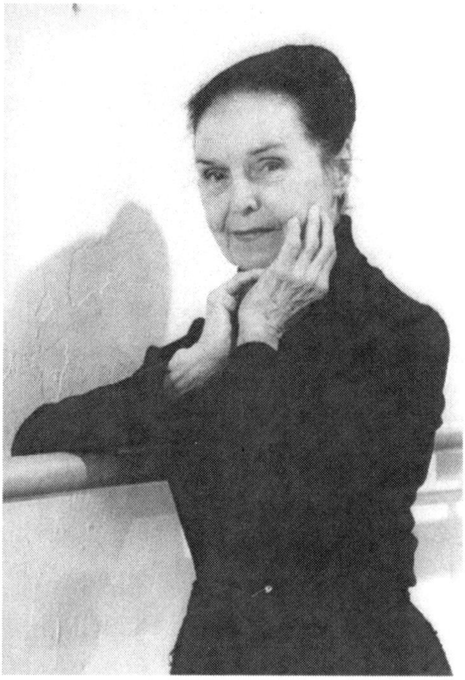

1. Agresta-Stratton, Abigail

Abigail Agresta-Stratton, MA, RDE
President, NYSDEA (NYS affiliate of NDEO)
3 Aztec Drive
Bay Shore, NY 11706

Thursday, September 08, 2011

Mary Anthony
736 Broadway, 7th Floor
New York, NY 10003-9519

Dear Mary,

I am typing this letter rather than writing it because you always told me that my handwriting was terrible and you were and are quite correct.

I want to thank you for allowing me to be a part of your studio and your company. I recall how excited I was at each turn of my career at your studio, from when I received a scholarship, to when I was made apprentice, to when you asked me to dance with the MADT at the Riverside Church, to when you asked me to dance in Ceremony of Carols, one of my favorite pieces.

When I was in high school, my mother drove me forty five minutes to Branford, CT to take a Master Class on a Saturday afternoon. My modern teacher insisted that I attend. My ballet teacher was angry that I would miss class. I never missed class. Well, not until then. I took your class and realized that ballet was not my calling after all. This was the way my body wanted to move! I was so intrigued by you and your technique! I wanted to learn more! That night, I saw your company, Phoenix perform. Weeks later, I went to NYC, for the first time, to take a class with you at your studio and was in class with Kristi Egtvedt when she first started dancing with Taylor. I came in again and years later, moved to the city and studied with you, and continued my journey.

In addition to dancing, I was Company Manager for a time and also Scholarship Coordinator for a longer time. Eventually, time came for me to end my daily classes and rehearsals and other commitments at the studio to teach dance full time in the NYC public schools. I came back occasionally. One day I came to take class and left afterward and did not return for quite a while, as I needed to go back to CT due to the illness of my father and both grandmothers. One day, I opened my mailbox and there was a letter from you, apologizing to me because you thought my absence was due to something you had done or said. The letter was so very sweet, so touching. I cried. I cried and I called and told you the real reason for my absence. You offered much needed support and love.

Another story that comes to mind happened the day after I performed in Ceremony of Carols. You came back into the dressing room, looking for me, because you needed to speak to me, so of course, I thought I was in trouble. You looked at me and said, "You were really quite good, but your bun was too low!" You proceeded to show me that my bun needed to be much higher on my head for this piece. I remember being both relieved and ecstatic from such high praise.

I use what I learned from you, about dance, other art forms, humanity and life in general every day as I am raising my own children and teaching dance, whether it be in a public school or in a private studio. Your work has had an incredible impact on me as a dancer, as a dance educator, as a choreographer, and as a person. I think of you often. I cherish the time that I spent at your studio and with your company, well, with your Theatre, the Mary Anthony Dance Theatre.

Love,

Abigail Agresta-Stratton

2. Blizzard, Mary Ellen

Who knows how deep the Heart is, and how much it holds.
— Emily Dickinson

August 22, 2011

Dear Mary,

"They can because they think they can". These words across an ocean scene with seagulls taking flight have become our greeting to one another. When I gave you this poster for Christmas in 1973, I would never have foreseen the resonance of these words in my life, and yours.

Mary, you have been my mentor, muse, and mother. My dance professor, Virginia Jinks, brought your company to Eastern Kentucky University in 1972. When I saw your youngest dancer, Gwendolyn Bye, perform in your dance, "Songs", I had to meet the choreographer who created such beautiful movement and imagery in such an exquisite piece. When you said to me at your master class the next day, "I'll know you when you plié," my course was set. I left college after my sophmore year and you gave me the first full scholarship that you had ever given a female student. As you whittled

page 2

my body with your vigorous and beautiful technique, you fed my spirit with art and a passion for living fully. Eventually, I would take the "great voyage of the soul" as you called it, so I could make peace with my childhood.

The Mary Anthony Dance Theatre was afire with creativity! Every class was a performance and if you dared miss a class, you might miss something to rival the concert stage! You might be tripleting across the floor with Ulysses Dove or trying to mimic the emotion that Clay Taliaferro released in every sinew of his body. Daniel Maloney, Ross Parkes, Yuriko Kimura, Sonea Shimin, Pat Kimi Thomas: your company is a Who's Who of Dance.

You gave us every possible gift, teachers such as the great Anna Sokolow for choreography class, Charles Moore for jazz, and the incomparable Mary Price for ballet. If you walked in the studio mid afternoon, Charles Weidman might be rehearsing "Fables of Our Time" or Anna Sokolow could be rehearsing "Dreams", imploring a dancer to be true to the movement.

Mary, you showed me the breathless mystery, sheer beauty, and uncompromising power of the sea in your masterpiece, "Threnody".

page 2

my body with your vigorous and beautiful technique, you fed my spirit with art and a passion for living fully. Eventually, I would take the "great voyage of the soul" as you called it, so I could make peace with my childhood.

The Mary Anthony Dance Theatre was afire with creativity! Every class was a performance and if you dared miss a class, you might miss something to rival the concert stage! You might be tripleting across the floor with Ulysses Dove or trying to mimic the emotion that Clay Taliaferro released in every sinew of his body. Daniel Maloney, Ross Parkes, Yuriko Kimura, Sonia Shimin, Pat Kinè Thomas: your company is a Who's Who of Dance.

You gave us every possible gift; teachers such as the great Anna Sokolow for choreography class, Charles Moore for jazz, and the incomparable Mary Price for ballet. If you walked in the studio mid afternoon, Charles Weidman might be rehearsing "Fables of Our Time" or Anna Sokolow could be rehearsing "Dreams", imploring a dancer to be true to the movement.

Mary, you showed me the breathless mystery, sheer beauty, and uncompromising power of the sea in your masterpiece, "Threnody".

page 3

I was privileged to understudy the Irish jig section of the dance. In dances you described as a painter limns, the rhythm of the sea in "Threnody", it's pull in "Tides" and the beautiful scallop patterns the waves make as they break onto shore in "Songs". I cannot be at the ocean without thinking of you nor can I resist doing steps of your choreography as the waves come in and out.

"They can because they think they can." These words have guided me through the solo dances I created until I was thirty, through my days as a chaplain, and now as a writer. Mary, you are never far away when I say these words to myself to buoy my spirits. I love you and you will be in my heart now and forever.

In gratitude, love and respect,
Mary Ella Blizzard

3. Boday, Mary Price

August 14, 2011
Dear Mary,

Starting "letters to Mary" has been wonderful for me as well as you. To see how you have touched so many lives is inspiring. You have always been the person I have wanted to be like.

I can still remember how we met. It was because of Darrell Barnett, the young man that I had taught before moving to New York City. He had auditioned for your company, and you quickly hired him, and you asked him who had trained him. When you learned it was Mary K Price who was a dancer in New York too, you invited me to take class from you.

Darrell Barnett and myself in June 1970 (just before moving to NY)

I took you up on the class invitation, and what a beautiful class it was. Lyrical, strong, meaningful combinations and steps put together are just adjectives to the incredible class that I experienced with you. After the class, you told me that you would like to hire me, but I was too tall for your company. And you generously offered me a scholarship to your school.

At the time, I was in the Lenard Fowler Ballet company, and I was under contract until the middle of November, plus I had already bought a class card at the Martha Graham School that had to be used up. The ballet company worked Monday through Friday from 9 AM to 5 PM, and I would go down to East 63rd Street to take the advanced Graham class.

In November, you telephoned me and asked me where I had been, as you had put me in the company, and the concert was coming up that you needed me to be a part of. You were preparing the performance at the Fashion Institute of Technology for December 20, 1970, and the rehearsals were just getting under way. It worked out perfectly, as I had just finished my ballet contract, and I was available.

The first rehearsal you had with me was on a Sunday evening with just you and me. I came into the entrance of your school and saw a poster on the wall for this upcoming show, and low and behold, my name was on it!!!

You were a dream come true! I loved dancing for you and being in your company of amazing dancers. Taking class before rehearsals was always inspiring standing next to Yuriko Kimura and Ross Parkes. Dancing for you were my glory years. That is one thing that is great about growing older. I can look back and know, what were the best opportunities I have lived, and Mary you were it. Thank you, Mary Anthony.

Love and admiration always,

Mary K (you always fondly called me by my Oklahoma name)

4. Bookspan, Audrey

9/19/11

Dear Mary,

You were my Dance Composition teacher at the New Dance Group in the late 40's — early 50's — a long time ago!

You gave me a life-long gift of your inspirational teaching. I composed a "study" based on the image of a tree with bent and twisted limbs. I called the dance "As the Twig is bent." Later on it developed into choreography to "Strange Fruit" sung by Josh White

And later on, it became part of my "American Trilogy"

1. John Henry - sung by Harry Belafonte
2. Strange Fruit   "   " Josh White
3. Bought me a Cat " " William Warfield
   music by Aaron Copeland

I want to thank you for giving me the tools for composition and choreography that reinforced my innate desire to tell stories through Dance

Audrey (Golub) Bookspan

5. Cohan, Muriel

Mary Anthony
Mary Anthony Dance Theatre
736 Broadway, 7th floor
New York, NY 10003-9519

Dear Mary:

How often do we sit down and write letters to people who have changed our lives? We always mean to... Mary's project provides us with that wonderful opportunity. I am enjoying the process of remembering my first studies with you, going back many years.

I was a student at the Philadelphia Dance Theatre starting at about age 14. Possessing a lot of passion and not much technical background, I was nevertheless included as part of the dance chorus in concerts all over Philadelphia accompanied by the Philadelphia Orchestra. It was a marvelous training ground with four powerful, dynamic teachers/dancers/choreographers leading the way. As part of our training, special guests were brought in from New York from time to time to give master classes. The classes were wonderful and I learned so much from all of these different perspectives. But somehow your classes were riveting. I remember being electrified by them, as they reached the very core of my being. I do not know how long it was after your first appearance that I began to make weekly trips to New York to study with you, nor do I remember how soon after that that I made the permanent move to New York.

I took classes with many wonderful teachers, but yours were the classes to which I kept returning. Perhaps it was your use of powerful imagery to get us to move in the desired way. Your literary and painterly stories and visions never failed to produce the right movement impulses, and to bring another dimension to the experience. Or maybe it was your amazing intuition about the needs and passions of your students.

When I finally became a member of your company in the 1970's some of my greatest hopes were fulfilled. To dance in such great works as <u>Threnody,</u> <u>Songs,</u> <u>Blood Wedding</u> and so many more, was an immeasurable gift. In addition, I met Patrick Suzeau, also in the company, who would become my dance partner and my life partner. Also, not surprisingly, some other company members and I formed life-long friendships.

During my time in the company you instituted two things which reflected a special openness and imagination. First, you invited your company members to choreograph and perform their works during some of your New York seasons. To perform in each other's works was quite enriching, and to have our own works performed was thrilling. Second, you invited other choreographers, contemporaries of yours, to set works on the company. Working with Anna Sokolow and performing in <u>Rooms</u> and <u>Dreams</u> was truly memorable.

When Patrick and I left the company to form our own duet company, your work, your teaching and your very being continued to inform us. The magic of your classes, your impassioned work and the generosity with which you shared all of this with us has marked me forever.

My profound gratitude,

Muriel Cohan

6. Cox, Anne

St. Luke's Episcopal Church

The Rev. Anne Cox Bailey
Rector

Box 2088
Walnut Creek, CA
94595
925/937-4820

July 23, 2011

Dearest Mary,

All that you taught me has stayed with me, informing my life and ministry wherever I have traveled. You gave me many gifts while I studied with you in the early 1980's: the gift of your dedication and experience as I learned new things about how my body moved through space; the blessing of taking as many classes as I wanted, including your lovely technique, Pilates and choreography; the great opportunity to work closely with you as your rehearsal assistant. There are words you shared that I remember still; gestures that spoke more eloquently than words; your love of cats, and the generosity of spirit that you have shared with so many, many dancers, professional and amateur. Under your caring, observant eye I became the best dancer I could be.

You gave me the ultimate gift when I could no longer stay in New York: a heartbreakingly lovely solo, and permission to teach your technique. You sent me forth with a glowing letter of recommendation that affirmed my abilities as no one ever had before. Dancers and audiences in Europe who would never have had the opportunity to learn of your supple, eloquent technique now know the name and work of Mary Anthony!

My professional dancing days ended, and a renewed sense of vocation arose, one I had tried to leave behind in my teenage years. As I raised a daughter, moved back to the United States and California, finished my undergraduate education and attended seminary, your instruction became metaphors — "the dance of Life" — offering comfort, strength and hope; people easily relate to dance imagery, and it helps them to understand their lives in ways they never realized before.

Now I am the rector of an Episcopal congregation, and as chief liturgist, responsible for the content and shape of the services. Sacred dance graces many liturgies (which are themselves dances) speaking to the community in ways beyond words, offering an *experience* of the HOLY that is grace-made-tangible: meaningful, cherished and remembered.

Thank-you, Mary, for all that you have taught me about movement, the Spirit, and Life!

With love and respect,

Anne +

The Rev. Anne Cox Bailey

7. Culley, Jane

August 12, 2011

Dear Mary,

  I'm writing this letter to thank you for the inspiration you have been to me both creatively and personally. As an actress I have learned as much from you as in any acting class, although the things I learned were in your amazing dance and choreography classes. Being in your presence has made me more humble and helped strip away the arrogance that often accompanies a lifetime of living exclusively in the artistic professional world.

  If I were to describe you to a young, potential student, I would say, "Mary teaches reality. She makes you see yourself for what *you* are and can accomplish – and if you stay with her, you will achieve the best of yourself. She will make you compete with yourself and teach you not to compare yourself with others. And daily you will grow and learn and learn to 'see' so that you can train the inner you (physically, mentally and emotionally) to fully express the creative soul within you to its fullest physical artistic expression."

  She brooks no prisoners. She is not kind, yet she can be gentle, while harsh. She will accept anyone, no matter what their limitations. Some adults run away in fear after the first class – if she feels they are not 'seeing' what they should attend to – or refuse to try out of fear of looking stupid. She will call them out in no uncertain terms saying "don't think – just *do*, like any five year old would do – 'see and copy!'" But, if they dare to enter her class for a second try, they will experience her magnificent gentleness and generosity as she helps them find out how to help themselves find their way.

  I am a far better performer as an actress and a dancer and a teacher than I ever would have been, had I not encountered Mary. I can't wait to run to class whenever I can just to be in her presence. We are all so blessed who have her in our lives.

  Thank you, Mary, for making me a better person and enriching my life on so many levels.

I love you,

Jane Culley

Jane Culley

> 8. Eshkenazi, Joan

Joan Eshkenazi
25 Middleway Circle
Forest Hills, New York 11375
Cellphone: 917 364 9836

September 9, 2011

Mary Anthony

736 Broadway

New York, New York 10003-9519

Dear Mary,

I was an insecure, nineteen year old when I sat on the stairs leading up to your old studio on Fourth Avenue. I had been told that you were "the best modern dance teacher in New York City" and your classes were physically exhausting, but, exhilarating. You arrived, and I knew immediately that I would be embarking on an exciting, new journey, forever enriching my life.

You asked me whether I aimed to be a dancer, teacher or choreographer. I had no idea as I was in love with dance in its entirety, but, you made me believe that whatever I wanted was possible. You offered me a scholarship and the studio became my second home. My painting, pottery and dance all became intertwined as life and movement infused each medium.

I remember the excitement felt when Cameron McCosh would place an iron on the piano strings to create the sounds of the Orient. The **inspirational music awakened the dormant creativity and the thrill of** dancing permeated the studio. I was thrilled to choreograph "The House of the Rising Sun" for your choreography class and still feel the excitement when I realized I achieved what I never believed I could.

You taught me sincerity in movement. Emotion and technique were inseparable. The contraction, so often misunderstood by others, was the core in your technique. So many others put emotion as secondary to movement. I recall how distraught you would become when the dancers performed without emotion. "Chutzpah," with a nod to the late Anna Sokolow, became part of your lexicon.

I am 72 now. As I look at my paintings and sculptures, I see the world of dance in them. Although inanimate, they move. You, Mary, are still part of my life. Shall we plan our next lunch date? There is still so much to talk about.

With love,

Joan

Joan

9. Gallant, Catherine

Catherine Gallant/DANCE 1623 Third Ave. New York, NY 10128

August 17, 2011

Dear Mary,

You are truly inspiring. Since first taking your class in 1979 I have had many teachers but none who generously opened so many doors for students. You always gave very freely of your vast knowledge of dance technique and dance making. I recall being stunned by the high standards and demanding expectations you held for all levels of students from beginners to your company members. This was clearly a way to set the path towards life long commitment to the art form and to the self.

You gave me some very important opportunities to create work and share it with an audience through your many studio choreography showcases. The space was sometimes tight and the floor made its own music but there was always a strong excitement and sense of possibility. Your direction and critiques were clear, insightful, and informed by a very keen sense of theatricality, musicality and openness to new ideas. You have a unique way of dealing directly and honestly with students without destroying the spark needed to ignite the imagination. This is the gift of your intelligence, perceptive skill, interpersonal expertise and deep artistry.

I always felt welcomed in your special space where the past, present and, most often, the future of dance came to exchange and share in your tremendous energy and radiant spirit. Personally I have always felt that you embodied the consummate artist moving forward with creating and teaching even when it was financially impractical and spiritually challenging. Certainly the dance world hasn't changed in those respects. The fact that I am still creating work against these many odds is a direct result of your tenacious and inspired example. Thank you Mary.

With respect, admiration and love,

Catherine

Catherine Gallant

www.catherinegallantdance.com

10. Gilchrist, Rebecca

"Don't look at the corner of the room - look beyond," you said. And so I did and I still do and I always will because of you.

To Mary Anthony

From Rebecca Gilchrist

In 1972, I moved to the Big Apple. That's right, New York City, the city of dreams and adventures. The first few months were rough, working in a crummy bar, too tired and dissipated to do anything else. I was stuck in a terrible rut - I moved to NYC to study dance and to audition for acting roles and here I was doing nothing.

Then all of a sudden everything changed. The bar closed with no notice and I was unemployed and finally able to pursue my dreams. First on my agenda was to find somewhere to study dance. Someone in my neighborhood, the Lower East Side, recommended Mary Anthony Dance Studio to me.

Mary's studio was on Broadway, just below 8th Street on the seventh floor of the building. (Pray the elevator is working.) I started with the beginning classes in Martha Graham technique as well as Mary Anthony's technique. The classes were revelatory for me and I flourished at the studio and began studying five or six days a week. Many of the classes were from Mary Anthony herself and I looked up to her as my inspiration.

After exercises done sitting and/or lying down, we then stood for feet and leg work in the middle of the floor before moving to one side of the room to move across the studio in triplets, runs, walks and leaps. Mary would exhort us to "not look at the corner of the room, look *beyond.*"

Mary said that even in winter, there are buds on the limbs of the trees just waiting for the sun to bring them to bloom. That we as dancers must always be growing, budding and giving birth to movement. Dance was not and is not a static destination. Dancing means to be in movement, even when one is still. How many, *many* times did I hear Mary say, "pull up, pull up!" She meant to pull up on the inside to keep the breath flowing in and out and to constantly pull the muscles up, fighting gravity every step of the way.

A "contraction" is a dance term that means that while exhaling, the area just lower than the navel is pushed back, back, back until it feels that the intestines and the belly button are pressing against the spine. A contraction is what makes dancers look so elegant, regal and well presented. When a dancer successfully contracts, there is a movement on the back of the body at the waistline. The contraction forces the middle of the back to expand out and up, all the time the tummy is pressed tightly back. Mary used to say that we should always in a 90% contraction - quite a challenge!

Mary Anthony is a small woman - around five feet tall and somewhere around 95 pounds, maybe less. She has always kept her hair long and jet-black. She radiates confidence and vitality and has a sharp tongue. She doesn't suffer fools gladly and has no patience for dancers who don't do exactly what she tells them to do. Mary established the studio in many years ago (I'm not sure when she started there) and had her own company for more than 40 years.

I started my danced studies there in 1972 and even had a scholarship briefly. However, paying jobs in the acting field eventually began taking me away from Mary Anthony. In 1978, I moved to Los Angeles and that was the end of my relationship with the studio.

Although I have studied at a number of other studios with wonderful teachers both in New York and Los Angeles, I have never had anyone who made more of an impression on me than Mary Anthony. I learned a lot about strength and vision from her in addition to dance technique.

In spring of 2004 I went to New York City for a theatrical opening and decided to investigate taking a beginning class at Mary's studio. The week before I left for NYC, I called and Mary Anthony herself answered! She assured me she remembered me, which was sweet and I'm not sure true, and told me that she was still teaching a beginning class on Monday nights at 5:30 to 6:30 PM.

I was excited and scared to death all at the same time. Although I do get regular exercise, it has been well over 20 years since I took a dance class from Mary and many years since I have taken from anyone else. I didn't even have a leotard and tights - so a trip to Capezio was in store. I bought the most traditional of footless tights and plain long-sleeved black leotard. (I wanted to look as if I had once danced.)

The experience was heady stuff. Mary was there when I arrived, sitting with her leg up on a sofa and actually seemed to remember who I was. She has some health issues - a knee replacement that isn't healing and is causing her discomfort. Her hair is still jet black and she is now in her late 80's! My eyes were wet with unshed tears the whole time I was in her presence. It occurred to me that Mary was about 55 years old when I began to study with her at age 22. At that moment, I was 56 years old, just about her age when I first met her. That she is still teaching is overwhelming to me.

The class was difficult but Mary praised and complimented me a number of times over the course of the hour. She held me up as an example to the poor hapless other beginners. There was one woman who was actually in my class way back in the 1970's. She still lives in her childhood home in Brooklyn and comes over to take Mary's beginning classes regularly.

At the end of class, Mary called me over and asked me with whom I studied with in Los Angeles. Of course, I don't study dance any longer so it was a lovely compliment. It is actually a testament to her that I continue to stay in good shape. Mary Anthony influenced me greatly and taught me much of what I practice on a daily basis, even though I no longer dance. I feel privileged to have studied with her and honored and blessed that I was able to take another class, more than likely the last one I will ever take again from her.

Thank you, Mary, for teaching me to look *beyond*...

Rebecca

11. Gottschild, Brenda Dixon, Ph.D.

Brenda Dixon Gottschild, Ph.D.
201 West Evergreen Avenue, apt. 615
Philadelphia PA 19118
Tel. 215 247 2974
Email. bdixongottschild@verizon.net
Online. www.bdixongottschild.com and fb

23 July 2011

Mary Anthony Dance Theatre
736 Broadway, 7th Floor
New York, NY 10003-9519

Dear Mary,

It has been long, too long, since I've made contact with you. I hope you will forgive me and understand how life sweeps us up and keeps us moving, moving, in its ineluctable flow. So I'm very glad that this invitation came from Mary Price Boday to send a letter to you.

I remember the last time we saw each other. It must have been ten years ago, at the memorial service for Rod Rodgers. It was a poignant but special moment for me to sit with you while we shared memories about him. Even then, I hadn't seen you in many a year. While we sat, waiting for our turn to rise and speak, we shared confidences as two women, peers, equals—a new development in my relationship with you. In the past I had been the ingénue, the protégée, and you my mentor. Time has an interesting way of seasoning our roles.

You were always so caring, so conscious of my needs—not only as a dancer but as a young woman struggling to find her way in the world. I hope you don't mind me saying, publicly, that in the early years after I moved away from home, you once or twice riffled through your closets and gave me wonderful clothes, knowing that I was living on a shoestring. I loved wearing your "stuff" and having a very sophisticated appearance for one who was in her early twenties. Earlier, when I went off to tour Europe after graduating from college (1963), you contacted a colleague in Paris and arranged that I could use her studio (on the Rue de Rome) for my rehearsals. Simply put, Mary, you took care of me in countless ways that went beyond your professional commitment to a promising young dancer.

Do you remember "Facciamo l'amore, non la guerra?" Make love, not war—that naïve Vietnam-war era saying was inscribed on an inexpensive pendant I brought back from Italy after my first (1968) tour with The Open Theater. Memory fails me, but I believe that we company members[1] had a more substantial replica designed for you because of your special love of and contact with Italy. Did we present it to you at one of our studio parties? A Christmas celebration, maybe? And when I left the Mary Anthony Dance Theatre to work full-time with Joseph Chaikin and his Open Theater, I recall you gave me a send-off party at the old studio (61 Fourth Avenue). And there was no hesitation, no holding me back, when I needed to move on to the next stage of my career.

In my third book, *The Black Dancing Body*, I single you out in the Acknowledgments, thanking you for valuing my dancing body and inviting me into the world of concert dance. With my desk scholarship and teaching duties, I was able to stay late and be one of the last people to leave the studio. In the early 1960s you and your Siamese cat lived in a very small apartment in back of the studio proper. And it was on a night that I was still on desk duty when you either opened the mail or received a phone call confirming a booking for the company at the Richmond (VA) fine arts museum. I remember you coming out from your apartment, saying that the booking was confirmed and, although you didn't know who (!!!) you would invite to dance in the ensemble, you would not be restrained by Jim Crow laws and would decline the booking if they did not allow African Americans. This was around 1965 and, indeed, I had hoped to be invited to perform—and I was. I remember the longish train ride from New York, the rehearsals in Richmond, and my awareness that I was the only person of color on that stage and that the audience was not integrated. This was a courageous stance on your part, Mary, and I'll never forget it.

And never will I forget dancing as the Cherry Tree in the lovely setting you choreographed for the Wakefield Second Shepherd's Play. Dancing in *At the Hawk's Well* and *Threnody* (as one of the three mourning women)

---

[1] Including, at that time, Lois Lowenstein, Barbara Leeds, Ellen Robbins, Ross Parks, and others whose names escape me.

was fulfilling, but the height of my Mary Anthony Dance Theatre experience was dancing *Songs*, with the wonderful John Parks as my partner in your ecstatic, lilting choreography. My feet barely touched the ground as I flew across the stage for those opening runs to the Debussy string quartet. It was my first (and only) dance role in which my partner lifted me. I was thrilled!

Mary, you may recall that I'm married to Hellmut Gottschild, choreographer and dancer in his own right. He was Mary Wigman's final assistant before he left Berlin to live in Philadelphia. We have a good laugh about the fact that I know all the Laban swings—thanks to your wonderful classes and the lyrical way you taught them to us—whereas he doesn't, in spite of his German background. I'm so glad you granted me permission to be lyrical and taught us that important historical material. And those swings, that lyricism, are still in my body! Moreover, you taught us Pilates long before it became a trendy fad. By your sterling example and the teaching opportunities you provided, you also taught me to become a thorough, observant studio teacher.

Dear Mary, you were my aesthetic mother, you know! How can I thank you enough for all that you gave to shape the person I have become? This letter touches only the surface of a deep well of memories. Bless you, for all that you mean to me and so many others. I treasure you.

Love Always,

Your Brenda

©Brenda Dixon Gottschild 2011. All Rights Reserved.

12. Hansson, Eva

Eva Hansson
188 Ave of The Americas #5FS
New York, NY 10013

Ms. Mary Anthony
736 Broadway #7
New York, NY 10003

October 30, 2011

Dearest Mary,

First of all, I'd like to thank you for all you've taught and given me over the past 9 years. Your words weren't always music to my ears but more importantly you were always right.

I still remember the first time meeting you, Ms Mary Anthony. Robert Diaz, whom I had randomly run into a windy and cold evening in NYC, and who continuously kept talking about you, introduced us. "I hear you want to join us" you said with a soft, sweet voice. A couple of months later I performed with your Dance Theatre for the first time in "The Seven Deadly Sins".

Your choreography workshops are very inspiring and your notes crucial in helping create visually dramatic dance pieces. Your teachings have helped me dramatize my own work and dances. You taught us to perform, to produce, to move into our characters; we became what we portrayed on a cellular level.

It did not take me long before I was taking your technique classes on a regular basis and you gave me a scholarship. You kept surprising me with more and more material. "How much is there?" and "How come I don't get tired of taking her class?" I was asking myself, getting stronger every day. Mary you always go beyond what is really possible.

Mary Anthony your exploration of movement and your choreography is astounding. Whether you are telling a story or recreating your surroundings with movement. This is always dramatic and precise. My favorite piece of yours both to dance and to watch is "Seascape". Possibly because I visited your beloved Fire Island with you once and the piece shows not only the beach, but also the feelings that are associated with it, including the sadness of having to depart after a joyful day.

You inspire me so much with your zest for life, and your ability to always have something positive to say. Your love and hospitality over the years has been immense. Not only did you teach, you also created a family around you with plenty of dance and holiday gatherings.
I am blessed to be part of this family.

Love,

Eva Hansson

13. Hayes, Linda (Harris)

Linda Harris
276 Prospect Place, Brooklyn, NY 11238 – home: 718.638.5865 – cell: 347.461.4695 – lindagharris@earthlink.net

Mary always reminded us to "smell the roses". "You're not shopping at Kmart." she would say while we were going through exercises in class, and she was often indignant about the so-called "progress" going on around her studio—in the world.

In fact, over the years, her studio, and her example, became an oasis that I returned to again and again. In my late 20's, very late, I came to dance enamored by music and movement and drawn to the purpose and discipline I noticed in dancers. Despite my relatively "old" age, I dedicated my life for seven years to serious training, even though a bad case of stage fright distracted me from performing. Nevertheless, dance became a major part of my whole life, and Mary has been a large part of that.

Mary was and still can be very hard on us, and sometimes even intimidating. I once summoned the courage to ask her opinion of my efforts to become a professional dancer. She curtly told me, "You had the talent, but not the drive". She had intuitively picked up on my ambivalence about a professional career, though we had never discussed it. Many years later she also showed her whimsical side when she said, "Why don't you just quit your job, Linda, and come dance!" That was during a brief period when I had been able to resume frequent classes, and she approved of the way I was dancing in class. She seemed serious and I was flattered, but I also thought it a strange remark as I was already past middle age and involved in another profession. Mary has always been a master driven by the purity of her vision and not life's practicalities.

More than that, even today, her studio (also her home, by the way) is a warm and casual place where the usual edge of competitiveness and rush doesn't intrude, as in many other dance studios in New York City. And the price! She has kept the price of classes extraordinarily low (even today a single class is just $10) and always was generous with work scholarships. This even though I suspect her way of living has been more modest than most people could tolerate.

When I was younger, the studio bustled with many talented dancers. Now, things are not so busy—but amazingly, Mary is still teaching us, with her constant talking through the floor work: "breathe in...breathe out". Her voice doesn't have the strength it once did, but seeing her there day after day (she is now 94 as I write this) is an inspiration. Teaching us is probably very difficult for her now, but also may be what she lives for.

Mary's studio has seen me through many of the markers of my life. When my daughter was born, I stopped dancing altogether for 10 years, but then, came back, for the sheer physicality and joy of taking class. When my brother committed suicide in the early 90's I blindly willed myself to class, and no one saw the tears as I performed the familiar exercises. In 2007, when my husband of 35 years died unexpectedly, I again found refuge in the familiar center of Mary's technique. My healing was connected to Mary's insistent quiet strength and discipline, and her complete dedication to beauty.

14. Jinks, Virginia Nill

September 9, 2011

Dearest Mary,

You have brought so much richness, joy and sunshine to my life. I truly feel privileged to know you. There are so many sides to you, Mary Anthony, in your thankfully long, inspired life.

It was a happy circumstance when I met Tom Wetmore who had discovered your teaching skills and recommended that I study with you. Tom, an English teacher, a near stranger and now closest of friends, decided that he wanted to study dancing and researched the then current teachers/choreographers that he admired.

So on my next visit to New York, I, a physical education major from Bowling Green State University, Bowling Green, Ohio who was fortunate enough to secure a position teaching dance at Eastern Kentucky University, Richmond headed straight for your studio. From the moment that I stepped onto the 7th floor at 736 Broadway, I felt that I had found a true warm, uncompromising home at personified by you, the teacher and artistic director. The classes were so much fun, so challenging. I believed that you cared about my progress and the progress of each of the students.

I began to look forward to my trips to New York and rarely missed a long week-end or vacation to come to continue under your guidance. As each New York visit came to an end, I left with great reluctance. Frequently I would start class even if I had to leave early to catch a plane — sometimes just barely getting to the airport on time. After a number of years I had a great opportunity — to take a semester sabbatical where I could come live in New York and live off my continuing salary.

Through your classes we learned not only the skills of a movement or theme, but we were advised about dance concerts to see, Broadway shows that excited, interesting museum shows. We learned to appreciate even more authors and poets, the beauties of nature, your concern for victims of injustice, the suffering in this world, your love of the sea, as expressed in several pieces of your choreography and your love for cats, especially your current studio cat, Tyger, thirteen pounds of golden haired curiosity. Currently he discovered how much fun it is to hitch a ride on your walker or that you are good for a generous helping of a special brand of cat treats. Always a great companion and always entertaining, it is interesting to watch as he leaps up on the desk facing the Broadway window. He pauses as if pondering the situation, then nimbly springs up to land on the expanse of wood wall that separates the office from the women's dressing room. He strides confidently down to the corner, turns and then halts before gingerly creeping across the curtain rod across the door. On his return trip when he approaches the starting point, he springs and plunks down noisily. Unfortunately he has not as yet learned from you how to land quietly, as a cat should.

Then, too, I recall so fondly occasions when I joined you on your week-end sojourns to Fire Island. There you retreat to your tiny summer rental, a very small guest house owned by a local realtor, Arden Catlin, who became so fond of you so as to turn over part of her home to you. On your trips out to Fire Island it was rush, rush, rush. Hurrying off the train at Sayville, running to Waldbaum to pick up a few items, and then racing off to catch the ferry. I, sixteen years your junior, could hardly keep up with you. You continually urged me, maybe nagged me, to move faster, to keep up. That is you, racing through life and thereby making your nearly ninety-five years crammed full of adventure.

Once at your retreat, we would pause and sit down for sips of a Pussy Cat drink before going our separate ways, you and Feline one of two Siamese cats and me to explore the beach and collect shells or maybe a rare find of some beach glass. Often we met later in the day for some coffee and cookies. Sometimes you would pick berries or beach plums in order to make your famous jelly. At least once, your catching poison ivy, which you said you never did, after recklessly tearing through the bushes to find the best fruit. You cooked the harvest up and brought it back to the city to add pectin to the cook down and top it with wax.

Along with your continuing interest in attending dance performances, you maintain your concern for the environment, world peace, animal rights, and of human struggles everywhere. Your determination and your struggles to keep going all show the mettle of your personality.

Through my years at Eastern Kentucky University, with the help of Skip Daughterty, Director of the Office of Student Affairs, twice I was fortunate enough to be able to bring your company to my campus to perform and teach classes. Some of the best dancers of the day were in your company, performing your beautiful and thought provoking dances, full of imagery. And so many great dancers have taken your classes. Your Saturday Advanced Class was like a Who's Who of the Dance World — Jimmy Truitte, Clay Taliaferro, Ulysses Dove, Daniel Maloney, Ross Parkes, and Thelma Hill. I hesitate to list anyone of the current dance scene in fear of omitting someone.

Obviously, I love you tremendously, a truly special person, a special teacher, a special friend and a lover of life, still exploring the world and amazingly enough being able to adjust/accept inevitable changes in your life. As you near ninety-five years of age, I can only reiterate that how grateful I am that you are still in my life after these many years.

With all my love,
Virginia Nill Jinks

15. Jowitt, Deborah

Deborah Jowitt
78 Christopher Street
New York, NY 10014
dj2@nyu.edu

Dear Mary,

The first time I saw you, you were onstage dancing. I remember it because I had seen very little dance beyond touring ballet companies and none since arriving in New York to join Harriette Ann Gray's company. Back then, dance companies tended to bind its members to them with steely ideological hoops: "We are the only ones working this way; no one else is doing anything interesting." In any case, we rehearsed almost every night, and none of us had money to spend.

It seemed almost heretical to go to the Brooklyn Academy (I think that was the theater) to see a concert by John Butler. I was dumbfounded. I had never expected that modern dance could be so so theatrical, so entertaining, so. . .well, sexy. I remember John and Glen Tetley in some sort of caveman number, fighting over, was it Mary Hinkson? I'd never seen a male modern dancer who could point his feet like Glen.

The friend I went with may have taken classes with you because she told me which one you were. I have a vision of you and two other women, romping around with joyful vigor in *Three Promenades with the Lord*, that piece with the folk-religious charm. Am I remembering it correctly? I can't see the other dancers in my mind. Only you. Not long after, I saw—and was powerfully moved by—your beautiful *Threnody*.

In the Fall of 1957, I got a closer view of you. I had auditioned successfully for Juilliard Dance Theater, then Doris Humphrey's project. But I'd had the meniscus in my right knee removed in early summer and no proper physical therapy afterward. I hurt it again almost immediately. Instead of getting back in shape in Juilliard's classes (large and intimidating), I took the advice of a friend: go to Mary Anthony's studio, she said; it's right around the corner from your apartment.

When I walked up the stairs to the little office area at the front, I felt as if I'd entered a family gathering. I'd never, in my limited experience, seen dancers so warm to one another and so fond and open with their leader. I can visualize some of their faces, recall some of the names. Paul

Behrenson, Joy Gitlin, John Starkweather, Bette Shaler. . . .The classes were demanding but joyful, because you made them seem like interesting adventures on which we had joined you.

    You asked me to be one of the women in *Threnody* for a concert way up north somewhere. Cameron McCosh may have been the fisherman son whom we women, in our shifting roles, both entrapped and mourned. You danced in your *Blood Wedding*. I remember not just the rehearsals and the performance (our lighting designer, Tom Skelton, was a terror!) but the epic drive back to the city. I had a dress rehearsal (maybe a performance) at the YMHA with Juilliard Dance Theater the next day. And it was snowing. Hard. We drove to New York City all night; you perched up front with the bus driver—talking to him, entertaining him, keeping him awake. A heroine. I felt guilty, as well as scared; was it just because of me that we didn't wait until the storm slackened? I never knew for sure. At dawn, we arrived home to sunshine and a silent city buried in snow.

    More guilt came my way. And embarrassment. And sadness. I missed performing *Threnody* in New York , because of a misunderstanding. You had a Y concert coming up in the spring. I was very busy with Juilliard Dance Theater and a troublesome love affair. I hadn't been to the studio and hadn't heard from you. I thought you didn't want me for the performance; you, it turned out, were counting on me. I had agreed to do a children's show on that date. I was furious with myself.

    In the years afterward, you always smiled and chatted when we met on the street.

    What brought our paths together again years and years later was *From the Horse's Mouth* and those gatherings of very diverse dancers. Sharing a dressing room with people you'd never dreamed you'd share a stage with is almost as much fun as finding yourself improvising with them in front of an audience. You and I had the good fortune to be together in the same cast for a whole week at Jacob's Pillow, where I could talk with you backstage and listen in the wings when you told your wonderful Irish story.

    I'm so happy there is to be a book about you. May it do you justice!
Love,

Deborah Jowitt

16. Knowles, Pat

September 2, 2011

Hello Dear Queen Mary,

In just a week, Mary and I will be with you in Philadelphia for the *Threnody* performance. Such anticipation! Looking forward to our dinner on Saturday and to meeting Ginny. I received a note from her yesterday telling me that you have been thinking about writing to me, but, you know, I feel your thoughts beaming in, so it's fine to just keep sending them through another dimension.

Ginny mentioned that she was at the University of Illinois in 1962 and danced in a piece choreographed by Willis Ward. Amazing how we're all connected by that place—Mary Price Boday, Ginny Jinks, you and me. It was Mary who told me what an inspiring artist/teacher you were when she was our ballet teacher in the 1970s. That led your many UIUC residencies over a twenty-year period.

I often get e-mails from alumni as far away as Australia asking about you and marveling at the fact that you continue to teach three classes a week, produce your annual *Ceremony of Carols* concert, perform intermittently in *Horse's Mouth*, set your works for international performances, and are now coaching the reconstruction of your *Threnody*. What an indomitable spirit you have, Mary, as you said in one of your notes a few years ago, "There are ups and downs, but I hang in there."

The department archives contain several photos of you teaching class and directing rehearsals, hair pulled back in a bun, wearing leotards and tights and one of your beautiful chiffon skirts—your passion, grace, integrity, and devotion to the art always shining forth. I've told many former students about having to buy a pair of tights so that you would allow me to take your class when I visited you in NYC a few years ago J. During that class, I thought that we may well be the only students in the world taking class from a ninety-three-year-old teacher who "dressed out," demonstrated fully, accompanied herself, and challenged us to the max.

You have given me so many treasures and cherished memories. I have saved the art calendars you sent me from MOMA each Christmas and the lovely handkerchiefs with lace made by your mother. Every time I pass the Erlanger House, where you stayed during all of your residencies, I recall your Urbana visit in 2004 when we had a party to honor Jack Baker, the architect, on the occasion of the 40th anniversary of the House. Your leg was in a brace and you had a bad rash on your face, yet you flew round trip from New York by yourself, "danced" with me in the studio, put on a lot of make-up for the party and looked fabulous, and gave an eloquent tribute to Jack at the event. And do you remember that magnificent sunset after a rehearsal for *Fables* on a frigid day in January, 1988? The world was silent and blanketed in white. We drove to the top of a hill in the farm area of the University, next to one of the round barns, and shared a moment of awe that I shall never forget. You have enriched my life, Mary, in more ways than you can ever know. My heart is grateful.

Love and sustaining grace to you, dear heart. See you soon!

Pat

17. Lowenstein, Lois

dear Mary,

The years in your studio were of the most creative, life giving years. They were years filled with classes, company rehearsals and life long friendships made and sustained.

One is fortunate in life to experience, to live with a master teacher. Mary you were this gift — your passion, your clarity, your skill and wide knowledge of literature and other arts, of life and your especial attention to the creative and emotional needs of your students — all this was a gift. I am ever grateful to you for these years!

There are precious few that give so much and have nurtured with so much generousity and rare skill the creative needs of so many students who came to you and continue to come. A master teacher taught me to think, to soar, to translate into movement life and it's many complexities. Your fierce insistence on technique but equally on movement that springs from the gut, the soul, are a legacy of your teaching. You choreographed some of the most beautiful and meaningful works. It was my good fortune to perform in your company and especially to perform a part in "Threnody" — your Masterpiece!

There was a unique quality to the environment in your studio. It was one of warmth and friendship. In terrible times, such as the assasination of President Kennedy and Dr. King, we all spontaneously gathered at the studio to do a class in respect, in memory. We understood each others need to express bare emotion in a class led by you.

And there was always music — the pianists helped

you leap and soar and stretch and bend and travel across the floor with such glorious feeling.

Indeed a studio that thrived with students from all over the world hungry for you to impart your image your skill, your movement. Indeed a gift to us all!

You are truly an insp inspiration to generations of dancers.

Always with love,
lois

18. Lyn, Janaea Rose

October 18, 2011

Dear Mary,

I am writing to thank you –
Not just for teaching me to be a dancer, a choreographer and an educator, which you did, but for teaching me how to live.

For modeling that the most important thing is to be a person of substance, with intention, discipline and accountability. To cultivate and value an accurate perception of myself, no matter how difficult, and to trust my instincts and deeper knowing.

When we first met and I auditioned for you, you said that I was already an artist but not yet a dancer. In that moment I felt truly seen - both for who I was and for who I could become with the right training and mentoring. You saw me as a true teacher does, without judgment and as a challenge in much the same way raw clay is to the sculptor. You gave me the tools to find and express my own voice in dance, not to become a brilliant copy of someone else.

You also taught me to never settle but to work to find a new language for each new piece of choreography, and for each stage of my life as an artist. That it *is* a life of work, of "joyous labor, undertaken with body, heart and soul."

You gave me patient hours of time during my graduate studies and we shared a love of Fire Island as a refuge from New York City. You followed my progress through my own companies and then in establishing myself in academia, staying in touch through letters that always gave me courage to continue whenever things were bleak and difficult. You always led by example and I strove to do the same for my own students and company dancers.

Recently, after I called to wish you a Happy 90th Birthday and was told you were unavailable, you sent me a letter saying that "whoever answered the phone could not have known how important it was to me, you are one of the ones who carry forward the work of Anna Sokolow and myself and that is very gratifying." I cannot tell you what that means to me and I am truly glad to know I have done you proud.

For myself, I know that who I have become as a woman and a dance artist is rooted in the deeply formative and intensive foundational time spent on the 7th floor of 736 Broadway. It warmed my heart to see you again onstage at the Joyce Theatre at the event honoring Martha Graham, and to see you being acknowledged for all the dancers you trained for her company. I am enclosing a copy of the photo we took together that day.

I am so glad a documentary of your life and work is on film now. I proudly show it in my classes, and am deeply honored to be a part of your living legacy.

So as simple as it sounds, my feeling could not be anymore heartfelt,
Thank you.
With love,
Janaea

19. Maloney, Daniel

Mary Anthony June 15, 2011
736 Broadway
New York, N.Y. 10003
AN OPEN LETTER TO A FEARLESS CHOREOGRAPHER – MARY ANTHONY

Dear Mary,

    There comes a time in anyone's life when certain things must be spoken to justify, acknowledge, and most of all, to celebrate the human condition. Fathers' advice to sons, Mothers' cautions to their daughters, Best Friends sharing heart to heart moments, Teachers' enlightenment to their students, and students paying homage to master teachers of art, and their experience of life, all qualify under "Words That Must Be Spoken."

    Over the 45 years I have know you, I have experienced many beautiful moments in your classes, dancing in your works, watching you perform, and watching other dancers bring your choreography to light. From being in your presence I have learned that choreography is at best only a set of instructions that dancers brings to life.

    From my understudy days in 1966 I saw that you came to rehearsals well prepared, and that made rehearsals a joy. You knew what you wanted, but were always prepared for the unexpected, when a mistake by the dancer made the choreography better that you originally intended. You made rehearsing a creative experience for all your dancers.

    What I loved the most about being in your classes were the many gazillions of themes for choreography you had, as we did our center work and crossed the floor. The movement of the planets, movement from The Purification, Songs of Innocence, Elvira Madigan, Blood Wedding, Women of Troy, Bullfighter Study, Primitive Study, Seascape and Threnody are just a few.

    I loved the way you taught and passed Hanya Holm's movement experience with Mary Wigman in your classes, while adding some of your personal teaching pedagogy as well. The whole Laban theory of circles, semicircles, ovals, figure eights, circles without changing front, and the lovely, integral arm movement that accompanied them were and still are, an invaluable tool to any dancer and budding choreographer.

    I was fortunate to see Gwendolyn Bye, who, as you know, now heads Dancefusion in Philadelphia dance what I thought was your ultimate female solo in "Seascape" with consummate grace and beauty. This stunning opening solo of a beautiful, flaxen haired woman dancing by the sea with sea gulls her only witness, to music by Dubussy remains vivid in my mind's eye to this day.

Mary, I didn't realize when I started writing that I had so much to say. I realize that I am no longer a young man, and you are even older, but I am revitalized just writing to you, about you. I will write again another day (I promise). Love you.

DANIEL

Mary Anthony
736 Broadway, 7th Fl
New York, N.Y. 10003
July 15, 2011

Hi Mary

Remember a few weeks ago I said I would write again and I am true to my word. I was going to tell you how I remembered my early classes with you on 4th avenue. I remembered being allowed to take the intermediate class, which allowed me to take classes with a number of Broadway gypsies who used that class as a warm-up before heading out to the theater. Such jetés I had never seen before as the "pros" engaged in a bit of friendly competition. I especially loved it when you let the class make up their own last 8 counts as they moved across the floor. We often were on the floor laughing at such outrageous combinations people made up.

James Truitt and Thelma Hill also used to take that class and it was such a pleasure to see two well known professionals do their thing in your class. One thing for sure was that everyone in that class respected you and I as a new dancer began to take measure of your statue in the dance community.

It is difficult to put it into words, but what I really got out of those classes was that the dancer became immersed in movement, which was immersed in beautiful line, and both the movement and line were deeply immersed in the dramatic intensity and intent of the combination.

I have been involved with dance all these years, and have absorbed certain things from certain people. From Anna Sokolow I learned the value of simple, almost natural movement and how deeply meaningful it can be. From Pearl Lang I learned the grand excitement and challenge of performing difficult passages of dance. From Martha Graham I learned the riveting power of stillness and the essence of dramatic timing. And from you my dear, how to become one with the music, drama, line, motion and emotion.

You are one of a kind. Love ya.

DANIEL

20. Mauldin, Deborah

September 28, 2011

Deborah Mauldin
260 Highway 83
Harpersville, Alabama, 35078

Mary Anthony
736 Broadway, # 7
New York, New York, 10003

Dear Mary,

You know that words inadequately convey how much I love you, for movement is the great method of communication of the depth and power the inner worlds and feelings. I always concentrated on that when in New York, and every dance I did there was for you.

It was really a miracle for you to come into my life – Many people led to finding you: the late, longtime ADG member Laura Knox encouraged my membership in the American Dance Guild in the 1990's, Past ADG President, the late Marilynn Danitz discovering in me a hard working, committed dancer and encouraged me to take up the ADG presidency in 2006, and *Voila* we met at the ADG Performance Festival!

It takes many teachers to make a dancer; I look back with respectful love to my teachers: Gerda Zimmermann when in college, Martha Wynne when I first came to Alabama…and more…but I had forgotten what it was to have a teacher after years of being a teacher.

What did you teach me besides discipline, respect, humbleness, strength, kicks and spit before going onstage, and fifth position plies? So much…you taught me about repetition: to run a Wednesday tech, Thursday dress, and to run and perform the entire show on Friday and Saturday (except for Sunday's performance when you just do the matinee and have a little party afterwards).

You taught me to forget dance studio rent and put my studio at my own house…you taught me to believe in my own talent, to not short-change myself just because I had been buried in a small town in the south, but to fulfill the imagination I was blessed with.

You have been the example that has made me a master teacher....I go into class now knowing exactly how to approach young bodies and minds: to master the class, to insist on detail, perfection, focus....to not be afraid of repetition...to be thorough and teach what I KNOW not what they THINK they want to do]

A class, any class, stops in utter respect when I lower my voice and speak or do as Mary Anthony would speak or do....I hope it is OK with you to emulate you so!

Marilynn Danitz told me that she knew we would get along because we were both spiritual, and she was right. The greatest dream was when (I follow and record my dream life), one night, I flew, in my spirit body, to your studio, and we sat on the windowsill of the first window in the studio and discussed the psychic depth of choreography.

It is very hard for me to not be able to come to New York and see you; to miss Threnody was inexcusable, but for the awful economy that leaves no money for travel...and I am so afraid that the next phone call or e mail will say that you have slipped away and are to be found dancing in the starry celestial heavens...and so, every night, from my station here on the planet called Harpersville, Alabama, I look up at the night sky and think "is Mary alive tonight? Is she sleeping right now, does she feel well...is she OK?"

I think that, cat-like being that you are, that you and the incredible energy, power and utter integrity of your being will go on - in eternity - through your soul, and - without doubt - through the hearts, minds and spirits of those who have known you.

My fullest blessings, hellos, tight hugs, love, memories of our fun forays around the block to get tipsy on martinis and have Japanese lobster soup or Cajun gumbo....laughing how you study the random gum prints of the beloved sidewalks of NYC, kisses to Virgie for BEING THERE for you during this summer and fall of 2011, raucous anticipation of your 95th birthday party in November, 2011, hoorays to Mary Price Boday for writing a BOOK about you, and my heart misses all my friends in NY on the ADG, Tina, Steve, Gloria, et all, - may we continue to be united in this wonderful family!

All my Love, All Ways and Always,

Deborah

21. McKinley, Ann

August 17, 2011

Dear Mary,

My memories of studying with you are as vivid as if it were yesterday.

I took classes from 1960 to 1971. The period of the 1960s was a magical time for dance in New York City. There was a flowering of the established dance arts, both classical ballet and traditional modern dance. It was definitely a "golden age." And there was a balancing surge of innovative work characterized by the Judson Church group, Dance Theater Workshop and dozens of other creative collaborations all around the city.

As a young dancer, I wanted to see everything that was going on and take classes with anyone who was teaching. In the course of my explorations I found your studio and felt I had found a "home."

At the time you were in the Fourth Avenue location near Astor Place. For me and many other dancers this studio was a sanctuary. The actual class room was not very large; but it had a special light and warmth. The shiny wood floor, the one yellow wall, and the antique embossed tin ceiling that resonated a sense of history made it special.

Your presence made it even more special. There was a sense of family. Unlike other studios, there was not a sharp competitive atmosphere. We were all friends who together practiced the art we loved in a supportive environment.

Of course, this atmosphere was engendered by you. Your style as a teacher was like that of a good gardener. A good gardener knows all her plants are different, each requiring different soil and different nutrients to fully blossom. You treated each student as an individual with individual skills.

For me one of the most valuable aspects of your classes was that each one was a beautifully choreographed unit. It was always a joy to *dance* your classes. Supported, as you were at the time by excellent accompanists, each class was a rich dance experience.

Dance accompanists are unsung heroes in dance classes. The repetitive nature of developing a technique in dance can quickly descend into drudgery without their musical support. During the time I studied with you, you had the best dance accompanists in New York City: Cameron McCosh, Jack Carter,

Shirley Gray, and Leonard Tuffs.

I can remember Cameron McCosh playing a ground bass with his left hand and the strings inside the baby grand using a comb with his right. These musicians supporting your teaching skills and choreographic excellence created a very magical time/place/experience in the history of modern dance.

One special example was a class on Good Friday sometime during the early 60s. It was an afternoon class at 3:00 and Cameron McCosh was the accompanist. You entered the studio and made a slight gesture. We understood you wanted quiet and that you would not speak. You demonstrated the class; Cameron played; we followed. Across the floor, you choreographed a progression of variations on carrying the cross. At the end of class you made another small gestured and left silently. No one clapped; we just walked out quietly. It was both an extraordinary dance experience and a solemn ceremony.

During the decade I studied with you, so many dancers who became well known in the field passed through your studio. Some were there for a short period like a rite of passage; others stayed for years. I'm grateful that I had the opportunity to be part of your studio and this magical time in dance history, working with a great artist.

With Love and Thanks,

Ann McKinley

Ann McKinley

22. Mitchell, Helen

August 1, 2011

Dear Mary,

I first heard of you when I was living in Paris and taking some dance classes in a large gymnasium filled with students of all abilities.

An American Tour Guide told me that when I returned to New York City, I had to study with only you and I would learn everything I needed to about dance. And so I did and what a great decision that was!

I continued my dance training with you for about 25 years — from the elementary level to intermediate to advanced. At this time I was still teaching in the N.Y.C. school system & would take classes in the late afternoon, early evening, & Saturdays. Soon dance became an exquisite form of inner wealth. One year I even resigned from teaching to study with you all day, every day. And so learning just continued on a deeper level and never ended.

I will never forget my wonderful dance memories, from the original studio on 4th Avenue to the present one on Broadway, N.Y.C. These classes were a very important part of my life, & I looked forward to your training, your wisdom, your wonderful stories, your elegance and dedication to each and every class

23. Pastorella, Andrea

Dearest Mary, 8/25/11

    I miss you. I haven't seen you in almost a month, which is a LONG time for us!

    This is a letter to let you know that I think of you every day and that I love you more than words can describe.

    Through you, as my teacher, mentor and lifelong friend, I have discovered myself as an artist, dancer, choreographer and teacher of modern dance. Choreography and dance are my soul's expression; those are what keep my flame burning and my desire to live. Not only have you inspired me on my path but also Josie, Stephen and many young dancers that I have brought to you for training and performance.

    The impact you have had on my life is tremendous- like dropping the pebble in the lake but your influence is larger than that because there are no boundaries to the impact you have on me and in the world. My first correction as a scholarship student was "you are not using your metatarsals" Mary, you are such a hawk eye! And I didn't even know what a metatarsal was then….

    Artistically your choreography touches me at the core. There is something so perfect in your craft and your choices of movement and music. The way you express through your work is deeply moving and masterful. It is an honor and a privilege to have your eyes on me as I work on a new dance. It is both exhilarating and intimidating. I am always surprised that each time over the past 30 years with you I manage to muster up the courage to show you what I am working on and then to wait for your feedback. Your brutal honesty, compassion and encouragement feed my soul like mother's milk to a baby. Speaking of babies I made my first duet with Josie in your studio when she was 7 years old!

    Your encouragement was so great that I then carried on having an intergenerational dance company, Movita Dance Theatre, for 15 years. We toured in Canada; performed for many years (and still do) in your wonderful choreography workshop performances we even made it to Lincoln Center- remember? I have made at least 25 dances over these years and I think I have shown you almost every single one; you gave me the gift of choreography. I watch you, I listen to you and I show you and I learn and learn and learn.

On a different note, I always like to remember all these years since (1994)I have given you massages; on the piano, on the floor, on Daniels very weird Physical Therapy table and finally on Daniels real massage table! I love to work on you and I know you love my massages. Really we are due for one!!

My darling Mary, no matter where I am or where you are you live in my consciousness, you are closer to me than my own breath. You are a wonderful and inspiring teacher, a masterful choreographer and one of the strongest women I have been influenced by! Thank you for your infinite generosity and love, for teaching me everything I know about dance, for your patience and lifelong friendship.

I look forward to seeing you at the Threnody performance on September 10th.

With everlasting love,

Andrea Pastorella

24. Phillips, Barbara Anne (Burns)

How Mary Anthony Changed My Life

I grew up all over America. The daughter of an Air Force pilot and officer, I moved as my father's career dictated – every year or two. We lived in more than 18 states, Canada and Germany by the time I was in high school. In 1950 while living in Texas, my brother, my sister, my mother and I all contracted polio. My brother was nearly paralyzed but made a complete recovery and overcompensated athletically for the rest of his life. My sister and I had some weakness and much greater limb asymmetry than is within normal limits, but no paralysis. To prevent scoliosis and future stunting we were sent off to ballet class in each and every place we lived. As it turned out I loved ballet. I loved to dance, to excel at it and loose myself in it. Sadly, I was never able to progress in ballet as we moved too often to make any real progress or go on point. One of my early teachers, a Russian expatriate, told me with great disappointment that it was a shame the goof-off of the class was the best and most promising student. I was hurt but we soon moved and I carried on goofing off in dance class as a matter of protection to dull my own disappointment and frustration at my inability to truly progress. I stopped studying ballet and modern dance when I graduated from high school and moved from California to NYC to work and go to college.

Life has a way of bringing you back to the things you love and after a hiatus of several years during college, when I was 20, I once again sought out dance. I chose to focus on modern dance because it was possible to be a serious modern dancer *even if you started late*. By late I mean after the age of 7. Living in New York City, I tried all the studios and after stumbling onto Mary Anthony's Studio – I fell in love with The Dance all over again.

Mary was the Modern Dancer Incarnate. She was beautiful, lithe, dedicated, determined and would counter only hard work and striving for excellence in dance and in her studio. If you were going to fool around, you had better fool around somewhere else. There was no settling for 2nd best in her world. Her studio was an oasis for me. Live piano accompaniment for class, a company of the highest caliber and professional dancers that were good people and amazing professionals. I felt as though I had found a home. For a girl who was always having to move and always seeking someplace she belonged – a home was my heart's desire.

Mary used to say, "Dancers are the luckiest people in the world because their work is their play." I was determined to really dance and was soon spending more of my time at Mary's studio dancing than at anything else outside of work. I was poor, young, and working my way through college at night, holding down 2 to 3 jobs at a time. I worked as a waitress, hatcheck girl, library assistant and any other job that would pay the rent and could be scheduled around my final year at Hunter College's night school and my beloved dance. It wasn't easy and Mary soon offered me a scholarship so that I could take as many classes as I could make it to and put me in some of her studio performances. Those scholarships were a God send as I was at last able to progress more quickly. I must say that I never became a professional dancer in New York City but I did travel to a workshop in Salt Lake City, was offered a place in the Master of Modern Dance program at the University of Utah and joined a company that toured the mid-west. I was within one semester of achieving my master's degree in modern dance when my life took an unexpected turn.

Mary showed me, by example, how to persevere, how to strive for excellence and never to accept second best. She was the consummate professional and held herself to the highest standard. She was unconcerned about wealth; she sacrificed all for her Art and Dance. In those formative years I looked to her for direction and guidance. I never found her wanting in ethics, integrity or honesty. Those years of study with Mary and her company laid the foundation for the years of study and dedication that allowed me to persevere 'against all odds' in the arduous path I chose after leaving the world of dance. You see, I fell in love with medicine as I had fallen in love with the Dance and went back to school at night to complete the pre-medicine requirements and apply to medical school. Everyone said I couldn't do it, as I was an OLD person. At the ripe old age of 27 a woman had little chance of getting into medical school in 1974. I used the skills and gifts I had learned at Mary Anthony's to keep my goal in view, to believe in myself and to ignore the physical discomforts inherent in the path I chose. I learned from Mary by example and through my own experiences in her studio that if you don't believe in yourself, no one else will and that no one can tell you to what heights you can go and what you can achieve.

So, thank you, Mary Anthony for all the gifts you gave me and the home you offered me in your studio and in your world.

Barbara Anne Phillips, MD, MPH, MBA
FAAO, FACS, FASRS, FWMA

25. Rosen, Bernice

                          Bernice M. Rosen
                          Apt. BA - 132
                          1609 Bayhouse Point Drive
                          Sarasota, Florida 34231-6768
                       941 966-1335   email: srosen5825@aol.com

                                                            December 31, 1998

Ms. Mary Anthony
736 Broadway
New York, N.Y. 10003

Dear Mary,

    It's so long since we've seen each other that you may not remember me. I studied with you many years ago at the New Dance Group and at Hanya's. More recently we spent an afternoon together at the Botanical Garden in Tempe, Arizona when you guest taught at Arizona State University.

    The reason for this letter is that I am editing an issue of Choreography and Dance, an international dance journal published in England, devoted to the New Dance Group. I would love to include photographs of either "The Devil in Massachussetts" or "Threnody". I never saw "Devil", but I remember "Threnody" vividly as a most powerful work. Would you be kind enough to choose which ever you would most like to be represented by, or which you think will reproduce best and lend me a copy for inclusion? I promise to be very careful with it and return it as soon as possible.

    Many thanks for your help.

    Warmest greetings and a Happy New Year.

                                                            Sincerely,

                                                            Bunny Rosen

                                                            Bunny Rosen

26. Shepard, Evelyn

Dear Mary,

How can I sum up in a few words all that you mean to me? Yes, it is Evelyn here, the one who always says "Do you know who loves you?" and you say, 'Who?" And I say, "I do!!" It was great to see you the other day for the Threnody open rehearsal, and to rehearse Gwen's company with you. I hope you will come to the performance on 9 September in Philly. I will be there.

When Pauline Koner sent me to study with you, I had no idea that I would be honed by a master teacher into a better instrument and taken into the company so soon. you have had a profound effect on my sense of self, of art , of ethics, of what it means to be a responsible person from the inside out!

One of my favorite memories is the time NYC was having a blizzard and I showed up for class. You gave me a private lesson and showed a side of yourself I had only seen in your choreography. It was that day that I realized what a gentle woman lived inside you. it taught me so much to see the softness; I understood so much more about being human after that special day.

What an honor and privilege it has been to perform your choreography. My favorites are the last movement of Songs and the lament in Threnody. From the rising circle embrace in Songs and the amazing Star of David unison section, to the eternal motion of the couples rocking arm and arm, stilling the star, looking to the future with hope and promise in their eyes.... and then to dance Threnody; and the chorus of mourning, universal rocking and pitching, tilted, as if tombstones on the hill. The final unison of the women full of tossing, churning like the ocean storms, thrashing in grief; and anger at God. To this day when I think back, being a body carrier in Threnody was one of my very favorite parts. A solo career is fine,and I loved it, but there is nothing like dancing in unison with humanity in a masterpiece by our amazing Mary Anthony !! I love you Mary!!

Love Always,
Evelyn Shepard=

27. Shimin, Tonia

Tonia Shimin
437 Reed Court, Goleta CA 93117

August 23, 2011

Dear Mary,

You are truly an indomitable spirit. From the time I first came to your studio where I was welcomed in for a Christmas party, through all my time with you as a member of your company, and then through our long chapter of making your documentary, you have been a true blessing and inspiration. A strong memory, that will always be with me, is of that moment when you entered to begin class, so full of intention. We all knew much was demanded, that we had to and would give our best, but it was also obvious that it was all in the spirit of the joy of dance and in the striving for the highest expression of the art. Thank you Mary for your guidance and for sharing your wisdom.

May your light shine on!

With much love and gratitude,

Tonia

Tonia Shimin

28. Smith, Ruel

Dear Mary,

First off I want to thank you for being one of the small group of immensely talented and very special people who have been instrumental in opening up the world of modern dance to me. Your classes, your teaching, your wisdom and your friendship have enriched my life in immeasurable ways, and your incomparable spirit and joie de vivre continue to be an inexhaustible inspiration. I also might add that you always referred to me as "one of the boys," and being so termed is a delightful thing at my age! As the smallest token of appreciation I want to share a memory with you that has buoyed my heart over the years.

Your spirit, energy and love of art in all its manifestations were all marvelously apparent one cold Saturday afternoon in February 2005, as you and I tried to find a cab after seeing the New York City Ballet at Lincoln Center. Our plan was to go crosstown to the Metropolitan Art Museum, as you had heard that from its roof garden there was a splendid aerial view of a portion of Christo and Jeanne-Claude's recently installed *The Gates* as it wound its way along Central Park's pathways. As it was just after the ballet had let out, however, there were absolutely no vacant cabs to be found in the immediate area so we began to walk east along 63rd St. toward the park. I recall that at one point along the way we did almost manage to get a cab, but in the end let a young mother and her small child take it instead.

As we came to Central Park West, with cars and buses, but no cabs, running down the avenue, we saw inside the park the deep saffron colored fabric of some of *The Gates'* panels rippling about in the stiff winter breeze. You immediately rushed for the nearest park entrance as I, hands deep in my pockets and head down to ward off the cold, tried to keep up with you. Plans had suddenly changed—rather than take a warm, comfortable cab across the park to the equally warm, comfortable Metropolitan Art Museum and view *The Gates* serenely from the museum's roof garden, you were now intent on following the meandering path of *The Gates* through the bitingly chill air as the art piece snaked it's way down to Central Park South, back up through the Children's Zoo and finally, two miles or so later, to the art museum. There was nothing I could do but to keep bundled, try to keep pace, and to marvel at your energy and enthusiasm for such a cold and physically demanding viewing of an art project that some New Yorkers would have preferred to see installed somewhere in either Connecticut or New Jersey.

As the winter sky began to darken we reached the museum, and you quickly went in to see if we could get to the roof garden while there was still a trace of light. Alas, however, the garden was now closed, and I eagerly suggested that we go to the museum's café to have a cup of tea and to rest a bit, as I was quite tired and in need of something warm to drink. You, though, would have none of such slack indulgence and suggested that since the museum galleries were still open for another hour or so that we should walk about and see all we could of the newest exhibitions. This we did.

Of course everything about the day was wonderfully satisfying, and the fact that I remember the experience so vividly even now is testimony to its place in the pantheon of culturally rich life experiences that I've had over the years. And that's the thing about you, Mary—you drive both yourself and all those around you passionately but kind-heartedly to deeply absorb, in the fullest detail and without pause, all the rich cultural and artistic experiences that life offers us, whether the experiences take place in your studio, on a stage somewhere around the world, or in a local park.

One more thing I should add. After the museum galleries had finally closed we stood on 5th Avenue for 15 or so minutes waiting for a downtown bus. One came and thankfully we found a couple of seats together—it was the first time we had sat down in the three or four hours since the ballet had ended. I was exhausted and wanted nothing more than to find a decent restaurant, have a leisurely meal, and then go home and sit and read until my bedtime. As the bus approached your stop near Astor Place, I asked if you'd like to have dinner somewhere in the neighborhood. You smiled sweetly, said how nice that would be but that you couldn't as you had a party you were going to later in the evening for which you needed to get ready!

With love, respect and gratitude,

Rene

29. Stone, John

Dear Mary,

In the nearly 20 years I have accompanied classes at the Mary Anthony Dance Studio, I have received an enormous amount of dance and life education, even though your pearls of wisdom were being directed toward dance students and professionals. It has been an honor and pleasure to be in the presence of so great a teacher and choreographer, a person of vast experience and knowledge who at 95 is still passionate about theater, dance, history, nature and art, and passionate about her students, no matter their level. You instill in your pupils a sense that art begins with technique, but does not end with technique; that we must express ourselves with clarity and purpose, and that the dancer must animate not only her body but her mind and face as well. Among the countless lessons I have taken home from participating in the Studio is that each day, no matter what is happening for an individual or in the outside world, we present our work as though we were performing on stage. You do not abide "going through the motions" or sloppiness, or anything less than the fullest effort: if one is conscious that class represents a stage that might be next month or tomorrow or today, one must raise oneself to the level of awareness, concentration and commitment appropriate for when an audience is in the house. When the dancers really absorb your message, and everything comes together, I feel I am witnessing more than a studio or a stage, but a sacred space of timeless art and beauty. I'd like to thank you, Mary, for the gift of your art and friendship.

John Stone

30. Suzeau, Patrick

Dear Mary,

We had our duet concert in Bangalore last week. Muriel did Meli Kay's Cinderella which you may have seen long ago. Meanwhile I did a string of short solos on Indian themes that are a fusion of Indian classical and modern dance, something that I have been exploring recently. To my relief it went well.

Muriel just returned to Kansas to work on her new choreographic projects while I came to Malaysia. Do you remember our Malaysian students Kooi Lan and Chi Pei? They performed in the University of Kansas production of Threnody. They send their regards. They are each mothers of 2 children remaining active as dancers.

In Kuala Lumpur I experienced tear gas for the first time in my life because of the demonstrations that went on along the lines of what is currently happening in the middle east. Now things are "under control" and I feel safe...

In Malaysia I am studying bharatanatyam with a superb artist, Shankar, trying to keep up with the constant changes that are occurring, and I am rehearsing for my next solo solo concert. I started working with a few good dancers in preparation for another concert and loving every second of it!
I enjoy the Indian, Chinese and Malay cultural mixture of Malaysia.

I joined the 21st century, bought an iPad and I am able to receive e-mails. Just on time to get one from Mary Price Boday, who told me that she is writing your biography. Tonia's DVD of you was superbly done and I trust that Mary Price will write with the same care and love as Tonia.

Do you remember that long ago you gave me a book of Buddhist mudras that I still have? Along those lines, in bharatanatyam, when the thumb and index fingers are joined together while the other fingers are spread it is called the swan mudra (hamsasya). With it, if you draw a line across your forehead it means destiny.....

I am so grateful that you went to Mexico and that they loved you there! It so happened that my first teacher (in Canada) Hugo Romero (from Mexico) was a fan of yours. He is the one who told me "you must go to New York, to Juilliard, but you must also study with a great artist and teacher, Mary Anthony." Would I not trust the man who, when I was 15 years old, changed my life by introducing me to dance?

When I arrived in New York, summer 1969, you were in Tanglewood teaching and performing. This was the summer when I had no place to stay. I slept in Washington Square or in Central Park, or when it rained between two doors as it was still possible then, when nothing was locked, on St.Mark's Place. I met you in the fall and wanted to take the advanced and intermediate class instead of the beginner's class. I wanted to grow quickly and you welcomed me in both classes. I paid for class that first day. It was an audition class. Unbelievably you returned my money and told me that I had received a working scholarship! I was elated! I grew so much as a dancer during that year.

Following a year of study with you and at Juilliard, on an impulse, having seen Indian dance, I left for India. With a little money saved from my Juilliard performances and my trip and rent covered by my brother I managed to study there for a year. Upon my return I was uncertain. Should I follow my love of modern dance or Indian dance? Again you welcomed me and the studio became my home, in every way, since you let me live there as well. What a great gift it was! I was able to concentrate fully on dancing.

Your classes were magical because they were imbued with poetry. Images were infused with each movement in order to give it phrasing. The technique was sound but it was about transcending it, so as to emphasize the dramatic and musical intents. And how rich an experience it was for me to understudy several parts of "Gloria," the lead female part in "Song" and the lead male part in "Threnody"!

I acquired a very strong technique (you called me once a pyrotechnician) and loved working on texturing movement, yet I was not performing. Some tall yet lesser caliber male dancers were joining the company. I was not. Therefore, when I was asked to return to Montreal and join a new company formed by Hugo Romero, I jumped at the chance. It was a great opportunity, with a contract that resulted in countless performances all over Montreal (dancing along with my friend Chris Gillis, who eventually joined your company) in works that I respected artistically, with the added bonus that they featured me.

A year later I no longer felt that I was growing in that environment because Hugo, for personal reasons, was ambivalent about keeping the company alive. The atmosphere not being productive, I jumped at the situation when I received a rather unexpected call from Pearl Lang asking me to join her company. I had never seen her work but it meant being back in New York, back to the Mary Anthony Studio with the ideal situation of being a student but also a performer. Again you welcomed me and soon after you asked me to join your company. You created a solo from "Ceremony of Carols" on me. Later on we worked on "Chasm" and I also performed in works of Daniel Malony and Ross Parkes. All were enriching experiences that led me into my own investigations as a choreographer, something I was eager to do.

The Mary Anthony studio was a place where harmony was sought; a welcoming environment, generous of spirit. Dancing was the essence of it. I was also surrounded by books (which I borrowed) and filled with music. I had the opportunity to observe rehearsals; I could watch "Threnody" endlessly. This is the piece I show my choreography students when addressing the perfect realization of an artistic concept.

Destiny, the swan mudra traveling across the forehead: you went to Mexico, then I met Hugo Romero from Mexico who led me to the Mary Anthony Studio where I met company member Muriel Cohan, who, during a MADT tour in Gorham, Maine (early 1970's) became my dear friend. Subsequently she and I became dance partners when I performed in her "Ooka the Wise" which you presented at the Theatre of the Riverside Church (1971 or 72?). She became my life partner following a Cohan/Suzeau 1973 tour of Mexico. It is with her that I formed our company and with whom, to this day, I choreograph and perform. You still inform our steps.

Dear Mary, with great admiration I remain forever deeply thankful for everything.

Patrick

31. Timm, Fred

Ftimm@verizon.net   **Frederick Timm, LMSW**   212-677-9792
535 East 14th St., Apt. 5E   c 646- 329-5226
New York City, New York 10009

August 15, 2011

Mary Anthony
736 Broadway 7th floor
New York, New York 10003

Dear Mary,

I'm blessed in you.

You fostered me in two significant ways – as an artist and as a person. For that, I am very grateful to you.

As you know when I met you in 1989 (me 41 – you 70 something), I'd already had a full career in modern dance, touring the world with Nikolais Dance Theater. That experience, though formative and fancy, left me scarred. I never wanted to do modern dance again – EVER!

Then, a friend said he had a great teacher for a beginning ballet class. I thought, Okay, I can do ballet. Sitting in the waiting room of your studio, someone said you won't need ballet slippers. Okay – barefoot ballet. Then the warm-up started on the floor and I thought, Okay, Zena Rommett has a floor-barre warm-up ... then it DAWNED on me. This is a modern dance class! Fate had fooled me – and I was loving it. Home again, contracting and releasing.

You asked my background and we realized we had common roots in Hanya Holm. I met her when she would occasionally teach class for Nikolais. And she had been your mentor. And as you had to break from her to find your voice and purpose, I had to break from Nik to find my voice – my purpose.

That first class, I realized you were a gifted teacher. Later, I discovered your dimension and depth as a choreographer. When you asked me to write the article for you for *Dance Magazine, Mary Anthony at 80*, I got to know you as a person and we became friends as you revealed your story. Through the course of knowing you, I became aware that you valued something that I did not always sense from my previous mentors – personal integrity. I found a teacher who, like me, wanted to find truth not only in art – but also in life, in daily living. We were a good match.

You fostered me as a dancer and I grew technically and expressively in your classes. You asked me to perform a few times in your company and I especially loved being Joseph in *Ceremony of Carols*. You taught me how to teach by example. I'm still stealing combinations from you for my classes. You got me a job at HB Studio teaching

Ftimm@verizon.net **Frederick Timm, LMSW** 212-677-9792
535 East 14th St., Apt. 5E c 646- 329-5226
New York City, New York 10009

movement for actors which led to my job at Nassau Community College. You supported my playwriting and you deeply respected and encouraged my latest venture as I became a psychotherapist. But most significantly, you fostered my being true to myself as a person. You spoke to me through your powerful example that to be a true artist, you had to be a true person. There was not only truth in the perfect gesture on stage but truth and integrity in daily living. True art nourishes true living nourishes true art ad infinitum.

One other thing. Anytime I think I'm too old to be dancing or daring or living fully and honestly and soulfully, I think of you and know I'm not too old. Around you, *too old* is non-sense. You're always a few years ahead of me dancing and daring, not giving in to the deadening pressures of cultural conformity or the comforts of unconscious living. When I want to "give up", I always remember that Mary's not too old and neither am I. Mary's still doing and daring – so can I!

One day you'll pass. One day I'll pass. But in the meantime, we'll live and dance and dare and live honestly, truthfully, vitally. The best answer to the mystery of death after all is to live fully the mystery of life. That's what you do – that's why I emulate you.

Blessings to you Mary. You're my teacher, my friend, my mentor, my inspired guide as an artist – as a person.

Love to you always for ever and ever,

Fred Timm

Fred Timm

32. Wetmore, Tom

August 5, 2011

Dear Mary....

I have been, like so many, blessed to have you in my life. I know you are aware that I love you and that I valued all that you taught me, but I don't believe you realize what a great impact you have had on me throughout my life. Let me explain....

I just went back through my old appointment books to find the date that I took my first class from you. It was on Friday, May 7, 1970, and it was, of course, an introductory class. I remember that I was very intimidated by the prospect of being in a dance studio taking my first class. I spoke to you briefly and told you I wasn't there to become a dancer; you smiled and said that was fine. I sat on the floor at the back and the class began....I can picture it so clearly now. The studio was very dimly lit with light from the windows only, and that had a settling effect on me. It was all about the sound of your voice and the drum, and I was drawn in. I was surprised that the pain I felt while attempting the stretches made me feel good; I know that I began that day to feel a connection to my body that I know I never had experienced before. I was so surprised by that and, as I walked off the studio floor at the end of that first class, I knew I wanted more.

In time, after months of classes, I realized that I was as attracted to being in your presence as I was to learning more and more stretches, steps, and combinations of movements. You had such a calming effect on me as I worked to get deeper into myself and the new connections I was discovering between my brain and my body. I didn't know where this was all leading to, but I knew that I was changing in ways I liked.

When I came to you, Mary, I was in a very, very unhappy and dark place in my life, and you showed me a way to get through and beyond it. Your classes gave me the most priceless gift I had ever experienced, something I never had sought to attain because I had no idea before I came to you that I could ever feel such peace within myself. You helped instill in me a confidence I had never had, and I have been deeply grateful to you ever since. I can never thank you enough for that.

In time, as you know, I decided that the struggle to teach English to 7th and 8th graders was no longer worth the pain it was costing me. I decided to teach dance. I wanted to attempt to reach students and change their lives as you had done for me. I so appreciated your kind support as I went to NYU and got my Masters in Dance Ed. Thank you for your encouragement. And I really loved teaching dance, especially to the beginners. Choreographing and performing with the more advanced students never excited me as much as guiding the ones who were just beginning. You see, over the years I most wanted to open doors to the joy of self-discovery through dance as you had done for me.

How can I ever thank you, my most special teacher, enough? You freely gave me your wisdom and your support and your guidance. You were a most powerful example of commitment to the task of daily challenging your students' creativity, and your work ethic inspired me with a model to emulate. And you shared your loving, generous spirit with the students blessed to be in your classes, in your presence. All of these blessings together made me a stronger person, more aware and appreciative of my surroundings, and a much, much better teacher than I ever had the hope to be.

Thank you, dearest Mary. And may God bless you.

With love always,

Tom

— Love,
Tom

33. Zema, Leslie

9/5/11

Dear Mary,

    I've sent you a copy of a poster that, of course, you know very well. I've enjoyed it for many years, all the years, in fact, since I saw your company perform in Waterville, Maine, where I attended college in the late 1960's. It's not surprising that with a picture of you hanging on the wall of my New York apartment, I should then enroll in classes at your studio.

    Oh, I was so new to the dance world in 1971 that I didn't recognize Jimmy Truitte when he came to your class one day. He came to study with a master teacher, and I was so fortunate to do the same.

    We've met each other over the years at dance concerts and you've always remembered my name. I am honored.

With gratitude always,
Leslie

Endnotes

1. Tom Wetmore "Childhood and Early Holm." (1974). Interview No. 1 with Mary Anthony in her 14th Street Apartment, New York City, November 22, 1974.
2. Hallie Flanagan's married name was Davis.
3. Walter Sorell, Hanya Holm (1969). *The Biography of An Artist* (Wesleyan University Press), pp. 12-13
4. Anna R Nassif (1997). "In Memoriam: Louise Kloepper," *Dance Research Journal*, 29(2): 130.
5. "John Cage: An Autobiographical Statement," accessed April 26, 2012, http://johncage.org/autobiographical_statement.html
6. Edwin Denby (1949). *Looking at the Dance* (New York: Popular Library) pp. 291-292.
7. Claudia Gittleman (ed.) (2003) *Liebe Hanya, Mary Wigman's Letters to Hanya Holm* (University of Wisconsin Press), No 2, page 100
8. Jack Anderson (1997) *Art Without Boundaries – The World of Modern Dance* (University of Iowa Press) p. 113.
9. Donald McKayle (2011). Telephone interview.
10. Alistair Maculay (2007). "Shakespeare's Scottish Dame: Ambition in Motion," New York *Times*, Friday, September 7, 2007, accessed April 20, 2012. http://www.nytimes.com/2007/09/07/arts/dance/07guil.html
11. Gwendolyn Jensen (2010). "Literature in Motion: Mary Anthony's Use of Shakespearean and Biblical Themes in Modern Dance," Master of Arts Thesis, University of New Mexico, Albuquerque, pp. 37-41.
12. "1949 Florida Hurricane" accessed April 20, 2012, http://en.wikipedia.org/wiki/1949_Florida_hurricane
13. Mary Anthony, personal scrapbook.
14. Olin Downes, (1952). "City Opera Troupe Gives Double Bill: Bartok's Bluebeard's Castle, Ravel's L'Heure Espagnole Presented by Company," New York *Times*, October 3, 1952.
15. Mary Anthony, personal scrapbook.
16. Tom Wetmore (1974). "4th Avenue Studio Years," Interview No. 5 with Mary Anthony's at her 14th Street Apartment, New York City, December 15, 1974.
17. Tom Wetmore (1974). "4th Avenue Studio Years," Interview No. 5 with Mary Anthony's at her 14th Street Apartment, New York City, December 15, 1974.

18. Doris Hering (1956). "TV: One Wonderful Sunday," *Dance Magazine*, pp. 25-29.
19. Mary Anthony, personal scrapbook.
20. Jack Anderson (1980). "The Mary Anthony Approach," New York *Times*, June 8, 1980.
21. Mary Anthony, personal scrapbook of old programs "1933 – Silver Jubilee Season – 1957," Jacob's Pillow in Lee, Massachusetts.
22. Mary Anthony, personal scrapbook of reviews (The New York *Herald Tribune*, July 4, 1957).
23. Mary Anthony, personal scrapbook of reviews (*Waterbury American*, July 3, 1957).
24. Mary Anthony, personal scrapbook of reviews (*The Berkshire Eagle*, July 3, 1957).
25. Selma Jeanne Cohen (1957). "Dance: Connecticut College Finale," New York *Times*, Monday, August 19, 22.
26. Mary Anthony, personal scrapbook of reviews, Margaret Lloyd, November 17, 1958.
27. Walter Terry (1958). "Variety in Modern Dance," New York *Herald Tribune*, December 7, 1958.
28. Mary Anthony, scrapbook of reviews (Mariruth Campbell, "First Lady"—"Arsenic and Old Lace," Nyack, New York, December 1, 1959).
29. E.W. (1960). "Mary Anthony Dancers In 'Superb' Performance," *The State Journal*, July 21, 1960. p. 3.
30. Tom Wetmore (1975). "Canzanissima," Interview No. 7 with Mary Anthony, Mary's 14th Street Apartment, New York, NY, January 1, 1975.
31. Josephine Fox (1965). "The day is mine, the land is mine, and no one can take it away," *Dance Magazine*, March, pp. 50-53.
32. Jack Anderson (1980). "The Mary Anthony Approach," New York *Times*, June 8, 1980, p. 17.
33. Frances Wessels (1965). "Mary Anthony Dance Theater," *Richmond Times*, April 24, 1965.
34. Tom Skelton (1956). "Tools of lighting design: Lighting a modern dance," *Dance Magazine*, March.
35. Dance Theatre Workshop (January 30, 1970. "Mondays at 9," 334 East 74th St, New York, New York.
36. Mary Anthony, personal scrapbook promotional package.
37. Tom Wetmore (1975). "Canzanissima," Interview No. 7 with Mary Anthony, Mary's 14th Street Apartment, New York, NY, January 1, 1975.

38. Eleanor Frampton (1970). "Dance Theatre Emotions," *The Plain Dealer*, January 25, 1970.
39. Trudy Goth (1970). "Mary Anthony Dance Theatre," *Dance News*, November 1970.
40. Doris Hering (1970). "Mary Anthony Dance Theatre," *Dance Magazine*, December 1970, pp. 76-77.
41. Don McDonagh (1970). "Anthony Dancers Use Bible Themes," New York *Times*, December 23, 1970.
42. This is the role that I danced for the grand opening of this new work. Although it was scary wearing footed tights with no shoes, I surprised myself when I was suddenly was able to do four modern dance tilt turns (penché in à la seconde) in the performance.
43. Anna Kisselgoff (1971). "Anthony Dancers Offer Six Works – Dramatic Emphasis in Program at Riverside," New York *Times*, December 30, 1971.
44. Don McDonagh (1971). "Anthony Dancers Depict the Nativity," New York *Times*, December 29, 1971.
45. Doris Hering (1963). "A Rest of the Stagehands and Ushers: City Center American Dance Marathon 1972 Spans Six Weeks at the ANTA Theatre," *Dance Magazine*, February, pp. 58-64.
46. Anna Kisselgoff (1973. "Anthony Company," New York *Times*, Mary Anthony's scrapbook.
47. Jeff H. Harvey (1974). "Dancers Display Abundant Talent," St. Paul Pioneer Press, January 14, 1974.
48. Chapter 4, page 56, (1953). "Fables For Our Time" choreographed by Charles Weidman, performed at the Ziegfeld Theater by the New Dance Group
49. Mary began calling the "Eve" portion "Adam and Eve".
50. Mary Anthony (1974). Choreographer's Notes, New York Public Library for the Performing Arts, Dorothy and Lewis B. Cullman Center.
51. Robert J. Pierce (1974). "The Mary Anthony Dance Theatre," *The Village Voice*, July 1974.
52. Don McDonagh (1974). "Anthony Dancers Bring Out Intensity of Strong 'Rooms'," New York *Times*, June 22, 1974.
53. Jennifer Dunning (1979). "The Dance: Anthony Theater," New York *Times*, June 18, 1979.
54. Susan Reiter (1979). "Mary Anthony Dance Theatre," *Dance News*, September 1979.
55. Jennifer Dunning (1980). "Dance: Mary Anthony," New York *Times*, June 19, 1980.
56. Constance Romero (1981). "Mary Anthony Dance Theatre," *In Step*, February 1981.

57. In 1974 Mary began calling Part 2 of *In the Beginning* "Adam and Eve" rather than simply "Eve."
58. Jennifer Dunning (1985). "The Dance: Mary Anthony Troup," New York *Times*, December 9, 1985.
59. Sarah Lyall (1988). "Dancer Is Facing Loss of Studio in New York," New York *Times*, January 12, 1988.
60. "The Martha Hill Awards," (2007) accessed April 25, 2012, http://www.marthahilldance.com/2394.html

Mary Price Boday, Master Teacher, Choreographer, and Dance Specialist, earned her Bachelor and Master of Fine Arts Degrees from the University of Oklahoma. Part Cherokee Indian, Mary danced professionally in New York City with Leonard Fowler Ballet, Mary Anthony Dance Theatre, Pearl Lang Dance Company, Larry Richardson Dance Company, and the Gaku Dance Company (Dick Gain, Dick Kuch, and Sophie Maslow). In Switzerland, she danced in the ballet companies of St. Gallen Stadt Theatre Ballet and the Zurich Ballet.

Her teaching experience includes Harkness Ballet, St. Gallen Ballet, Zurich Ballet, University of Illinois, David Howard Summer Workshops, Mercyhurst College, Illinois Ballet (artistic director), Oklahoma City Ballet, and Oklahoma City University.

Mary's has choreographed for Harkness Ballet 2, St. Gallen Ballet, University of Illinois, Mercyhurst College, the Illinois Ballet, Opera Illinois, and Mary and Friends.

www.marypriceboday.com